Garden of Virtues
Planting Seeds of Goodness

by Christina Keffler and Rebecca Donnelli
Illustrated by Suzanne Etman

Thomas More Publishing
An RCL Company
200 East Bethany Drive
Allen, Texas 75002-3804

Bookstores: Call Bookworld Companies 888-444-2524 or fax 941-753-9396
Parishes and Schools: Thomas More Publishing 800-822-6701 or fax 800-688-8356
International: Fax Thomas More Publishing 972-264-3719

Printed in the United States of America

Library of Congress Catalog Card Number 99-85802

ISBN 0-88347-449-2

1 2 3 4 5   04 03 02 01 00

Dedicated with love to our parents, our husbands,
and the source of our inspiration, our children:

Abby, Joey, Sam, Ellie, and Will Keffler;
Jessica, Emily, Ben, and Hannah Donnelli;
Nicole and Natalie Etman

We gratefully acknowledge the earnestness of:
Lisa Dunn, Nancy Brown, and Deanna Albrecht;

the fortitude and generosity of:
Cathy Little Dannelly of 3D Production;

and the patience of our friends at Thomas More Publishing:
John Sprague, Debra Hampton, and Angie Kilroy

— Chrissie, Rebecca and Suzanne

Table of Contents

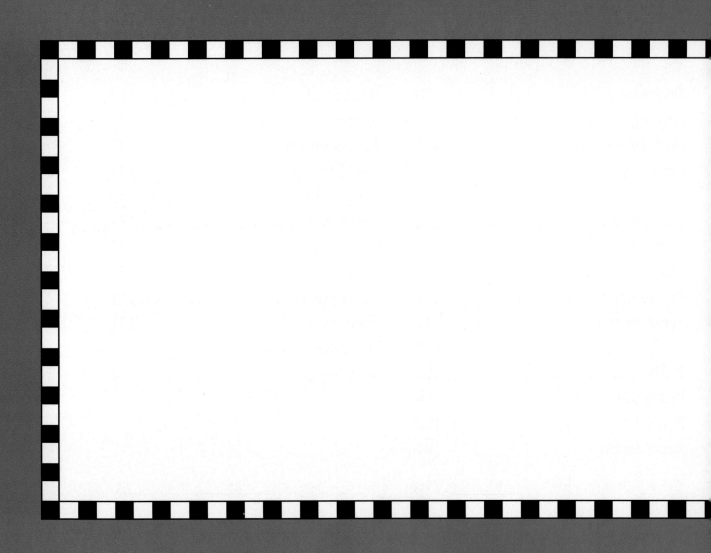

Introduction

Witness a mildly fearful five-year-old climbing a dark stairway chanting, "Fortitude. Fortitude," and you realize that virtues are empowering. As responsible parents, we realize that our most important job is to raise children with high moral purpose. In the garden of life, the seeds of virtue are to be planted early and in good soil. The soil where the seeds grow and eventually blossom is the family. Our continuing attention to the growth of the seedling virtues is the water they require to sustain life. The time to plant the seeds of virtue in the child is from birth. But planting requires careful tending over the years as the seeds grow and break through the soil of daily living.

Using This Book

Garden of Virtues: Planting Seeds of Goodness offers parents a guide to instilling in their children a commitment to virtue: explanations of 53 important virtues, examples of how to practice them, motivation and implied suggestions for cultivating them, and reflections on family life. The virtues treated in this volume are not presented in a suggested order of importance, but only in alphabetical order. Parents may, therefore, read and reflect on them, and converse with their children about them, in any order they please; the essays on the virtues do not build one on the other. Perhaps the order may be dictated, in part, by the children's behavior. The only requirement in this regard is to deal with all of the virtues over a given period of time.

Special attention should be paid to the opening page of each chapter, where the art continues the theme of seeds, planting, and cultivation, and where the virtue is

defined and three practical suggestions for family life are suggested: Positive Habit, Break a Negative Habit, and Family Rule.

The fact that there are 52 virtues, plus one to grow on, suggests that you consider having a new virtue for family consideration each week of the year. Depending on the children's ages and capabilities, you might encourage them to make a poster or other graphic about each virtue—including the Positive Habit, the Negative, and the Family Rule—and post it on the family bulletin board.

You will, like any farmer, have to engage in this important parental role of instilling virtue with a good deal of patience, satisfied with a long-term outlook, slow progress, and occasional relapses.

It is recommended that parents have an occasional chat, planned or spontaneous, to blame or to praise, with one or more of the children, reminding them of family rules and generally motivating them.

The Virtuous Life

Striving to be good for goodness' sake is the sum and substance of virtues. Traits and attitudes that are practiced regularly for the good of others and ourselves rise to the level of virtues. In ancient Rome, the word *virtus* described the firmness and solidity with which a man conducted his public and private life. It carried the notion of bravery, strength, capacity. The Greek word for virtue implied a certain noble-mindedness. Religious philosophers have held that virtues are a reflection of the image and likeness of God. Nonreligious people in pursuit of virtue are motivated by a humanistic sense of ethics. Virtues, deeply held religious beliefs for some people and pragmatic standards for others, are enduring qualities of one's character by which a person is enabled to live morally, to act in praiseworthy ways.

Practical reasons for being good, or virtuous, abound. Channels of love, virtues give human beings an identity. When we are virtuous, we lead more meaningful lives and are better liked. Virtues help us to be more effective human beings, higher achievers. The virtuous person, then, is likely to enjoy higher self-esteem and more likely to avoid the unpleasant or tragic consequences of unvirtuous deeds. Virtues improve our lives; without them society would be unthinkable. Life is more peaceful. In the worst of circumstances, a virtuous frame of reference will compel us to search out the greater good. When challenges, disappointments, or misfortunes befall us, we can better cope, adjust, and survive.

Noble, upright reasons for being virtuous are a requirement for a personal quality to be defined as a virtue. If we are religious, our Creator expects of us virtue based on good intentions. When we do things for the right reasons, for goodness' sake, the results can elevate the quality of our own life and of the world.

Vices of any kind are the weeds in our garden of virtues. They have taproots that grow downward and deep. It's not enough to pull out the weeds of vice. We have to go a step further and plant seeds of goodness that will grow into virtues and eventually crowd out the weeds of evil.

Habit is an essential element of acquiring virtue. To get to the point where we act morally without thinking about it is the ideal way to be virtuous. When children are learning to tie their shoes or ride a bike, they must focus totally on the task at hand. In no time, though, can they do these things while daydreaming about the upcoming game or why bees buzz. But it takes practice. Being virtuous becomes second nature, done in the rush of everyday living, only after it has been practiced and becomes deeply rooted.

People need a moral authority, someone or something outside themselves to guide them, if they are going to pursue the virtuous life seriously. Admirable people can help us to be objective about our decisions and behavior and motivate us to pursue the high road. People who are religious have an advantage in this respect in that all religious faiths provide moral guidance. Part of this is providing a moral role model, who may be a member of one's religious tradition, a historical figure, or, of course, a family member.

Everyone, but especially children, needs a nurturing relationship that inspires them to give the best they have to offer; they need a role model to stimulate their desire for the virtuous life. It does not matter if we are rich or poor, brilliant or average, talented or unskilled; we are all equally capable of it. History has taught us that human beings will pursue their hearts' desire at any cost. We have to work at making sure these desires are directed to high moral purpose. Planting and cultivating seeds of goodness in our children will result in virtue—in full bloom.

The Secret of the Garden of Virtues:
The Cardinal Virtues

Every good gardener has special tools and tricks of the trade that make the job easier. The gardener knows that some spindly plants need to be staked and that you need to have the right amount of water—not too much, not too little. For the gardener—the parent, really—the secret of the Garden of Virtues is the cardinal virtues.

Faith, hope, and charity, theological virtues, are gifts from God. The human virtues must be taught and learned. Among them are four cardinal, or main, virtues: prudence, temperance, justice, and fortitude. On these, all other virtues are hinged (the basic meaning of "cardinal"). Understanding the meaning of these four virtues and how they relate to all other virtues is the secret of the garden.

• Prudence, which is the virtue of reason and judgment, provides objectivity. A prudent person understands the concept of his or her actions and their consequences.

• Temperance is the virtue that provides balance and moderation. It bridles our passions and appetites.

• Justice is being righteous in our dealings with other people. It helps us to give others their due, to live out the "golden rule."

• Fortitude is courage. It catapults us into necessary action or holds undesirable impulses firmly in check. It is endurance to get a job done.

Here is an example of the relationship of these virtues to another virtue: orderliness, or time management. Suppose a man feels as though his life is falling apart because he is overcommitted. Temperance helps him notice his life is disordered with excesses. He thinks it through prudently and decides that some activities have to go. Justice helps him keep the needs of others in mind as he alters his schedule. Fortitude helps him get beyond pride and say "no" to certain demands where "no" needs to be the answer.

The cardinal virtues are needed in their own right, but still in relation to other virtues. They help us practice the other virtues in the most loving way possible. As soon as we disregard one or the other, the human virtues become unhinged and everything falls apart.

When parents feel confused about a course of action concerning the family, the "cardinal check," described above, is recommended to help them discern what to do.

One other virtue stands out in the garden: humility. Requiring realistic self-knowledge, it has been called the foundation virtue, the mother of all virtues. If we want to be receptive to moral training and if, as parents, we want to be a moral guide and teacher, we have to be humble. If we don't know who we are, if we don't honestly recognize our strengths and weaknesses, we can't move beyond ourselves to cultivate our cherished garden.

Audacity

Forging ahead with passion and against all odds to carry out a noble venture of great magnitude

SEEDS TO PLANT:
Consider your full potential.

WEEDS TO PULL:
Don't discourage the dreams of others.

FAMILY RULE:
Act with gumption.

Initially, I was surprised to find "audacity" on a list of virtues. How many times have I reacted, "Well, of all the nerve!" or thought, "He has a lot of audacity to do that!" I thought audacity implied that someone had overstepped conventional bounds in a shameful way. Audacity does mean stepping out of line, but in a determined way and for a noble purpose. It's what my mom calls "gumption." We can also think of it as daring, pluck, courage, boldness, valor, fortitude.

We are capable of much more than we realize. We underestimate ourselves because we tend to be shortsighted, lazy, or lack self-knowledge or self-confidence. To acquire and nurture audacity, we need to recognize our full potential and be convinced that some goals are eminently worth our effort and, indeed, demand our effort.

Before we set out on an audacious course, we must be well informed and aware of the consequences. If our goal is significant and upright, then we proceed in spite of the risks or even the likelihood of failure. Familiar with the way the world works, we have a warehouse of knowledge to draw upon, which will help us predict outcomes or foresee obstacles in our path; it will allow us to avoid pitfalls in our struggle for a better world, for the fullness of God's reign.

We can also act with others for an audacious purpose. The Magna Carta, which is the foundation of most democratic legal systems, was forced on King John of England in 1215 by a group of like-minded noblemen. Because he was given no choice, King John signed the document under duress, giving his subjects more freedom. Over five hundred years later, another band of single-minded individuals with a noble aspiration signed the Declaration of Independence.

Thomas Aquinas said, "Audacity increases with good health, energy and youthfulness." We need to be prudent about our health so we will be able to fight the good fight when we are presented with a virtuous proposal. We need to bring our children up to believe that they can, with audacity, make a difference. And even if we don't have objectives requiring audacity, or "gumption," we can help others who are striving to do good and are open to the risks.

Raising moral children is itself an audacious undertaking. At times, society seems to confound our efforts. But with passion and with audacity, we can maneuver around the quagmire of society's questionable values and teach our children the difference between right and wrong. If we persevere, remaining audacious, we can succeed against all odds.

Chastity

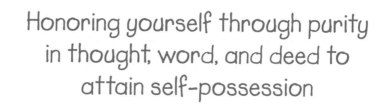

Honoring yourself through purity
in thought, word, and deed to
attain self-possession

SEEDS TO PLANT: Watch uplifting movies.

WEEDS TO PULL: Don't be swayed by the opinions of others.

FAMILY RULE: Choose happiness over instant gratification.

C hastity" sounds so Victorian, suggesting distaste for our very healthy human sexuality. Chastity—which is not the enemy of sexuality, but its partner—is commonly mistaken for suppression and restriction. It is a virtue that ensures freedom. Chastity is bigger than sex; it goes beyond control or restraint of sexual desires. It involves an attitude of reverence for one's body and for sexuality itself. Instilled as a virtue from childhood, it soars with genuine self-esteem. It should be the goal of all people, married and unmarried alike. It makes self-possession a tangible reality because it keeps us balanced and whole, which in the long term is our best hope for happiness.

Chastity protects the innocence of our children. The lack of chastity in our society has defiled our culture and sullied our sensibilities. Children are entitled not to be oppressed by blatant expressions of sexual freedom. The entertainment and advertising industries, on the whole, have little interest in promoting the ideal of developing a chaste way of life, and far too many parents have given up on the ideal.

Who hasn't heard a parent say something to this effect: "Of course I don't want my daughter to have sex, but the likelihood of it is so real that I want her informed and protected"? Can you think of any other immoral or undesirable behavior that a parent will yield to by alleging helplessness? With the possible exception of underage drinking, even the most permissive parent will step up to halt, by any means available, drug use, suicidal behavior, and criminal actions.

Try to imagine how you would react if a parent proposed the following: "My Annie wants more money and has decided to rob a bank. Now I don't approve, mind you, but what am I going to do? I don't want her to get killed if she tries it, so I'm going to buy her a bulletproof jacket."

No rational parent would ever entertain such a thought. A loving parent would throw herself between her child and any destructive element coming her child's way. Yet we easily surrender our children's fragile psyches and tender bodies to the so-called pleasures of the flesh because we throw up our hands in the fear that unchaste sex is "inevitable."

Thankfully, most of us have no fears that our children are going to rob a bank. From a very early age, we have told our children that stealing is wrong. We made a fuss when they came home with someone else's toy or shoplifted a package of gum. We told them that stealing was against the law, leading perhaps to a criminal record that would limit their future.

There will always be slip-ups and mistakes. Parents can do all the right things and still see a beloved child turn away from chastity. I'm not suggesting that it is the end of the world. At the very least, it's sad to see something as precious as virginity tossed away. Once virginity is lost, it can't be reclaimed, but chastity can be reclaimed, and this should be recognized. Chastity is a channel for peace and long-term personal satisfaction. It is the best way to avoid heartache and to look forward to a life filled with options and promises.

Compassion

Understanding another person's pain
and suffering and being willing to help
Believing you can make a difference
in the lives of other people

SEEDS TO PLANT: Serve others in time of need.
WEEDS TO PULL: Avoid being self-centered.
FAMILY RULE: Be passionate about caring.

Have you ever taken a few minutes to study a picture of Mother Teresa of Calcutta? There is a picture of her on a book that lies on my coffee table. In this picture, her eyes seem too big for her diminutive face and her hands too large for her tiny stooped body. Is this because she saw more pain and suffering in this world than most people do? Did she need extra large hands to lovingly touch the suffering people she served?

We need to be vigilant, sensitive to the suffering of another. Seeing a person's pain serves no purpose if we don't do what we can to alleviate it; that must be our abiding desire. But our compassion needs to be in keeping with prudence, justice, fortitude, and temperance. Prudence should direct our compassion so that we take reasonable steps to eliminate or lessen the cause of suffering, mindful of the victim's long-term good. Justice bids us to do more than be concerned about the cause of suffering, to the neglect of the one who suffers. It requires fortitude to stop collaborating somehow in a drug or alcohol abuser's habit. It is intemperate to want to end suffering by ending the life of the one living in pain.

Another form of compassion is to let people be compassionate toward you. About six years ago, one of my dearest friends, Terry, started feeling bad. This energetic mother of three little girls began experiencing a variety of physical ailments. She saw several doctors who treated her symptoms but had trouble coming up with a diagnosis. It eventually became clear that Terry had ALS, or Lou Gehrig's disease.

When a devastating disease strikes a beloved friend, sister, daughter, mother, and wife, there is a clarion call for compassion. Terry's extended family, her church, her school community, her neighborhood—we all looked for every possible way to show our love and offer support. Meals were provided three nights a week, car-pooling was extended, the three daughters taken care of, a visitation schedule arranged.

Terry's husband, Dick, took such tender care of her it was painful to watch. One of the first things she lost was the ability to speak. We all tried to read her lips, but no one could do it like Dick. How often we needed him to interpret what Terry was trying to say during our visits.

But the most compassionate person throughout the ordeal was Terry herself. We all needed to feel that we were doing something for her, and she let us do it, no matter how humbling it was for her. She knew how hard it was for us to visit her, and she made the visits uplifting by being her usual funny self. When I left her house, it was always with the sound of her voice and laughter playing in my head, even though she could not speak or laugh out loud. When people talked about how saintly Terry was, she got madder than a wet hen. She didn't want to have ALS, didn't want to be helpless, didn't want to leave Dick and her girls, but she couldn't help being com-passionate. She let us fuss over her, cry for her, do for her, and pray for her. It helped the people who loved her survive the disease she couldn't. As time heals all wounds, the compassion Terry showed us lingers and makes our healing possible.

Conscientiousness

Letting your moral sense of right and wrong
be your guide in every thought, word, and deed

SEEDS TO PLANT:
Examine your conscience daily.

WEEDS TO PULL:
Don't disregard guilt.

FAMILY RULE:
Let your conscience be your guide.

You may recall how Jiminy Cricket defined "conscience" in the Disney movie Pinocchio. He said it was the still, small voice inside us that tells us right from wrong. Starting in the sixties, the notion that conscience is an indispensable guide in determining the morality of an act began to go downhill. People everywhere seem to have worked to stamp out guilt as if it were a deadly disease.

Guilt is to the soul, my sister Terrie tells her four girls, as pain is to the body. If you are doing something that makes your leg hurt—stop doing it. If you are doing something that makes you feel guilty—stop doing it. What happens if you're in training to jump hurdles? You work to overcome the pain and eventually you can tolerate more and more physical strain. That is fine in the pursuit of physical fitness, but training your spirit to disregard guilt could land you in serious trouble. We should respond to an awareness of guilt like we would to cold water hitting us in the face. Our goal should not be to get past the guilt, but to avoid doing what causes it. Guilt is a wake-up call that we are morally accountable.

If we want to become more virtuous, then we have an obligation to develop an informed conscience. "Conscience" comes from a Latin word that means knowledge within oneself. We can't just look around and take a poll and decide that because most people are doing something, then it must be okay.

One way to determine if a behavior is immoral is to use the cardinal test: If an action can't be called prudent, just, or temperate, then a little fortitude is called for in avoiding it.

Do we sometimes have unjustified guilt feelings? Sure, and my mom always called this being scrupulous. It is misdirected guilt. An example is feeling guilty about being happy while others are unhappy. It might come from an inability to forgive yourself, which is as wrong as withholding forgiveness from others, assuming you have made amends for what you have done.

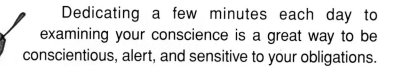

Dedicating a few minutes each day to examining your conscience is a great way to be conscientious, alert, and sensitive to your obligations.

Resolve to improve your moral acuteness each day. At the same time, look for ways to be more informed about what is right and wrong. The more highly developed our moral sense, the better we act. Too often, for me, it is like a new exercise routine. I start out firm in my intentions and then get distracted or become lazy. If only I could hire Jiminy Cricket to be my personal trainer. . . .

Constancy

Being steadfast in mind and spirit, regardless of circumstances

SEEDS TO PLANT: Be consistent.

WEEDS TO PULL: Don't contradict yourself.

FAMILY RULE: Make sure your actions are consistent with your beliefs.

My mother is an enigma to me to this day. But if I could have chosen any mother in the world, it would still be her. She is in her late seventies, and I still treasure every minute I can spend with her.

Mom is not, and was not, like June Cleaver or Donna Reed. Oh, she never worked outside the home, her house has always been immaculate, and she bakes great cookies. As a matter of fact, I don't recall ever not having dessert after dinner. Sound like the perfect mom of the fifties sit-coms? Not exactly.

My mom has a temper. When I was growing up, she yelled a lot. If you believe in stereotypes, you might say my mother has a typical headstrong Irish disposition, which means she has screamed a lot. Once I read a movie review about *The Quiet Man*, starring John Wayne and Maureen O'Hara. At the end of the review the critic said, "I just wish I knew what Maureen O'Hara was so mad about all the time?" One might pose the same question about my mom.

The funny thing is my five siblings and I were always rather indifferent about mom's temper when we were growing up. She was just being mom. As we look back, we roll with laughter at some of the things she would say—or yell. We even made a list of her famous sayings and put them in a fiftieth wedding anniversary book we made for our parents. Here are some samples: "Blessings? I'm supposed to see you as blessings? What did I do to make God so mad at me?" "You're going to get tuberculosis if you don't . . . put on some slippers . . . drink your orange juice . . . get to bed at a decent hour . . . come in out of the cold." "You want to climb the roof? Are you crazy? I don't have time to sit at the bedside of a vegetable!"

I guess you could say she was steadfast in mind and spirit regardless of circumstances. My father teases her by saying he married a woman with an even disposition . . . mad all the time.

Balance the above with the fact that if a blizzard blew in, Mom would be at the door of St. Maria Goretti school with an armload of coats and blankets and a box of canned food.

No, you won't find any Jerry Springer segments with my brothers or sisters or me. In spite of my mom's "high spirits," she was, and is, the most singularly devoted human being I have ever known. A volatile temper in no way indicated an unevenness of attachment or commitment to her family. Her constancy in doing good far outshines any defect of personality or temperament. My father, my siblings, and I were, and now along with our children, are her constant preoccupation and she blesses us still today.

Cooperation

Relinquishing control and sharing your skills generously with others

Working toward a common goal

SEEDS TO PLANT: Give up control.

WEEDS TO PULL: Don't be a slacker.

FAMILY RULE: Share the love, the work, and the load.

S ometimes there is no greater good than to declare a state of emergency and call for a whole house pick-up. When we were really busy and orderliness had gone out the window, we would declare a time-out. Everyone would stop what they were doing and help put things where they belong. When things were at their worst, this could take up to forty-five minutes. For me this was a last resort, for my kids it was a preventive measure. They were trying to prevent the "dreaded rampage." All this happened years ago, but the memory of it still haunts them.

The children were playing with every toy in the house, in every room, at the same time. The house looked like a police search-and-seizure operation had just taken place. I was just starting to pick up, and with the task before me having been so over-whelming, I'm ashamed to say, I lost it. I yelled and threw things, and I even cried. I was so out of control that I went to my room and slammed the door. I have a vague recollection of the look of shock on their little faces. After composing myself, I stepped back in the living room.

They looked at me with an expression that said, "Who are you and what have you done with Mom?" I calmly began to explain myself by saying, "You have just witnessed a rampage. Do you know what a rampage is?" One of them said, "Yeah, it's something that buffalo do." After I stopped laughing, I gave them their first lesson in cooperation, which they still think of as "rampage prevention."

Putting our entire house back in order is a crystal-clear exercise in cooperation. It's giving up individual control. No one is allowed to whine, complain, or argue. We are on a mission to pick up everything. To whom it belongs and who got it out is immaterial. If you can carry it, reach it, or drag it, you put it away. Slackers will be consigned to hard labor and will have to do it all by themselves the next time. Within the hour, everything is in its place and life can begin anew.

Cooperation makes this work. Sometimes we divide and conquer. Sometimes we move from room to room like a vigilante clean-up crew. We all serve as pack mules. As we leave one room, everything that doesn't belong in the room gets properly replaced as we move through the house. We all feel a sense of satisfaction and peace. Is this giving the kids a lesson for life, or what? They know the meaning of cooperation!

Detachment

Resisting social pressure and
materialism in order to fix the
desires of your heart on righteousness

SEEDS TO PLANT: Choose consequential over inconsequential.

WEEDS TO PULL: Don't buy all the latest gadgets.

FAMILY RULE: Be in the world, not of the world.

A t first glance, the definition of this virtue sounds "highfalutin": an attitude or perspective that liberates us from an imbalanced or disordered relationship to a person or thing. The decision to attain the spirit of detachment in our lives requires us to reevaluate how prominent and even how dominant we allow things to become in our life.

I'm not suggesting that we need to sell everything we own and live off the land somewhere. Anything that is not indecent is fine as long as we are moderate with our time and attention to it. Leisure activities, hobbies, athletics, and spectator sports are morally neutral. Home decorating and electronic gadgets are, too. If we use these things to relax or enhance family life, they are good things. We just have to make sure they are not ends in themselves.

The Pokémon craze has hit my house. In the past we have also had Ninja Turtles and Nintendo crazes. None of these things of themselves bother me. However, I was more guarded about how much time was consumed playing with them or thinking about them, because this preoccupation crowded out time for other equally good or better pursuits.

Adults are just as vulnerable as children in becoming too attached to worldly things. Like children, we are left with less time to spend on more worthwhile things. When I was a little girl, my father took up golf for a few months. Even though he enjoyed it, he dropped it because it took up too large a chunk out of his Saturdays. With six children, he couldn't afford that much time in a private pursuit. He picked it up again after retiring and is enjoying it now without feeling guilty.

Being habitually trivial in our pursuits distracts us from more important matters. Every single thing we do does not have to be of great consequence, but being single-minded about a trifling pursuit does not leave much time for what is upright and honorable.

When we are detached from worldly things, we can be more objective. We can stand back and see things as they really are—separate from our feelings about them. This helps us develop sound judgment, which is necessary if we are going to have our hearts fixed on righteousness.

Discernment

Making an important decision, drawing a profound conclusion, or taking a course of action after deep consideration of right and wrong and after seeking moral counsel

SEEDS TO PLANT:
Consult your moral authority.

WEEDS TO PULL:
Don't forget the cardinal virtues.

FAMILY RULE:
Right makes might.

When we use the virtue of discernment, we are not talking about what to have for dinner, where to go for vacation, or even what to major in at college. Discernment is reserved for big decisions that have implications of right or wrong that aren't always clear. Discernment is for when we are standing at a crossroad. It is prudence with an attitude.

Discernment, a process of making a prudent evaluation requires methodology. It's advisable to have a model to work with when going through the evaluation process. Certain steps can guide us to make a good decision and enable us to avoid complacency.

Step 1: Write down all possible solutions or options and their consequences. Be thorough, consulting with people whom you admire and who have had similar experiences.

Step 2: Pray if you are religious.

Step 3: Narrow your list of options by eliminating any that are unrealistic or clearly morally unacceptable.

Step 4: Review options again and delete solutions that will affect others unjustly.

Step 5: Seek counsel from someone you believe to be a moral authority, but not someone you can count on to say what you want to hear. Moral authority should be impartial.

Step 6: Let your conscience be your guide. Make certain your conscience is informed. Avoid wishful thinking.

Step 7: Come to a decision.

To double check your decision, use the "cardinal check." Have you left out any compelling facts or consequences? Can you live with the long-term consequences? Is the decision a temperate one? Will it result in upheaval for anyone involved? It's possible that a certain amount of upheaval will result in any case, but is it manageable? Does the solution or course of action you have chosen ensure justice for all concerned? People, including yourself, may not be happy with your decision, but ultimately you have to follow your conscience. No decision that is intrinsically evil is morally valid, and is therefore out of the question.

After you have determined a course of action, use all the fortitude you can muster to proceed. Find people to support you in doing what is right. You will always find it available from like-minded people and from God.

The peace that comes from making the right decision or choosing a moral course of action will strengthen you in your resolve. "Right makes might" is a truism that will serve your cause for a lifetime.

Earnestness

Trying your hardest to do your best in every endeavor

SEEDS TO PLANT:	Give it your best shot.
WEEDS TO PULL:	Don't settle for mediocrity.
FAMILY RULE:	Strive for excellence.

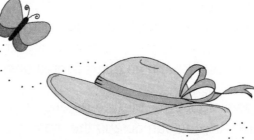

Seeing a preschooler seriously trying to make his bed is an inspiring thing to watch. He'll undo one end trying to tuck in the other end. Not to be discouraged, he'll crinkle his little brow and eventually use his whole body to get everything where it's supposed to be. Regardless of the final outcome, his sense of satisfaction at seeing the job finished will fill him with pride. "See what I did?" he'll say, not noticing the crimps, wrinkles, or unevenness, and you will agree that it is the best made bed in all the world because earnestness is irresistible.

When I was a schoolchild, my parents could overlook a poor academic grade, or forgive an occasional slip-up in conduct, but they wanted to see a perfect grade for effort every time. They knew that the habit of trying our hardest was, in the long run, the most important thing we could learn. There would always be people to help us when we fell short academically, and no child has perfect conduct all the time, but a genuine effort overall ensures a bright future.

Earnestness, or persistence, or stick-to-it-ness, is seeking to do things as well as you can. It's the most anyone can do and the most anyone can expect. Doing a job halfway or doing it poorly just so you can say you did it is not earnestness. It's one thing to fail, but to fail to be earnest is to be an underachiever.

When I was single, I had the opportunity to be involved with a Special Olympics event. When I watched these mentally disabled youngsters bear down upon the physical challenges presented them, I witnessed an exalted form of excellence beyond anything I could have imagined. They were able-minded and able-bodied in a way that most mentally and physically healthy people only dream about. The breadth of their earnestness was a vivifying sight to behold.

The insightful and witty British writer G. K. Chesterton is reported to have said that if something is worth doing, it is worth doing poorly. Now that may have its own version of truth, but as a guide for life, it is open to misunderstanding and falls short of the resoluteness we need to give our best effort in all we set about doing.

Faithfulness

Staying true to your beliefs and ideals,
regardless of circumstances
so that your beliefs are reflected in all
your relationships and in your
thoughts, words, and deeds

SEEDS TO PLANT: Cling to principle in small matters.

WEEDS TO PULL: Don't deny your beliefs.

FAMILY RULE: Believe in something.

*E*very meaningful facet of our lives craves faithfulness, demands it if it is to have lasting significance. If we are faithful to our beliefs, we will live them. If we are faithful to our ideals, we will have direction. If we are faithful in our relationships, they will be deepened and be increasingly satisfying.

Life can be so hard. We have so many reasons to be discouraged. Discouragement preys on us because of our little private pitfalls. It corrodes our collective spirits as we watch incomprehensible acts of hate across the country violate our sensibility. Our culture bombards us with "reasons" not to be faithful, not to be people of our word. Whatever happened to "my word is my bond"? Broken promises, violated treaties, dishonored oaths—the cynical faithlessness of society leave us gasping for something pure, something reliable and binding, despite inconveniences.

Very early in life, most of us heard the parable of the prodigal son. If you have ever looked up the word "prodigal," you might have been surprised to discover that the parable is very much also about a prodigal father. The first negative meaning of prodigal is "wastefully or recklessly extravagant." The second is positive: "giving or yielding . . . lavishly abundant." Prodigal in the positive sense is so big and bountiful that it's hard to get your arms (and heart) around it.

For most of us, God is the prodigal father when it comes to faithfulness.

Saint Augustine turned a clever phrase when he said, "Faith is to believe what we do not see, and the reward of this faith is to see what we believe." His observation can be applied to our faithfulness. If we are faithful to our relationships and to virtuous objectives, we will see in others and in ourselves what we believe to be meaningful and true.

Fecundity

Being fruitful or receiving the fruitfulness of others for its inherent value

Love not for reward or personal gain

SEEDS TO PLANT:
Give generously.

WEEDS TO PULL:
Don't contradict a compliment.

FAMILY RULE:
Enhance life with love.

Purposefulness is a good thing. Making sure our life and decisions have well-meaning intentions is the purpose of this book. Here we have a virtue that helps us to not always have a purpose. How confusing!

I have only heard "fecundity" used in the negative and in relation to panda bears. Ling Ling and Sing Sing could not fecundate. The meaning of fecundity—related to "fetus" and "fruitfulness"—is to be prolific, to produce new life. Having and raising children is an act of fecundity but it's only virtuous if we do it fearlessly. I, for one, face fear in regard to child-rearing almost daily. Renowned spiritual author Henri Nouwen has said, "When fear dominates our lives, we cannot quietly and patiently protect that holy space where fruit can grow." If I am trying to develop the virtue of fecundity, then I must try to let go of fear for the future. True fruitfulness gives us hopeful expectation about the future, in part because of the gratitude we feel for the gifts we give and receive in the present.

I should do things for people and expect no reward. I should also let other people do for me and feel no sense of obligation to them for their kindness. The late Mother Teresa is a role model for fecundity, which is ironic because her every action had great purpose. She didn't do what she did for any purpose except love, and love is revealed in her fruitfulness. She also enjoyed fecundity because suffering people were able to heap their love and affection on her when they had nothing else to give. This allowed them to have fecundity. Life enhancing life.

We should strive to encourage fecundity in our homes. Children need to know that they are valued simply for being. Sometimes we forget to let them know this because we are so busy directing them toward achievement. If we would be conscientious about showing love for them with lots of hugs, kisses, words, and time spent being together, then we should allow them to give it back to us, even though that's not why we love them.

Almsgiving is something we do for charity. Based only on love of another and expecting nothing in return, almsgiving requires no receipt, no tax write-off, and, for the most part, no notice. It can then be received without a sense of obligation or humiliation. Imagine that you are walking down the street and come across a blind man selling pencils. You put some money in his tin cup and you don't take the pencil. Wrong. You should take the pencil, but not because you paid for it, since that would negate the almsgiving. You take the pencil because not taking it implies that the blind man has nothing to give. Fecundity is life enhancing life.

Flexibility

Appreciating the thoughts, opinions, and behavior
of others without compromising
your principles and beliefs

SEEDS TO PLANT: Respond positively to the unexpected.

WEEDS TO PULL: Don't insist on your own way.

FAMILY RULE: Take things in stride.

Virtues are probably the least politically correct thing in the universe. We live in a time of "whatever" and "no rules," as the popular commercial says. Flexibility is not about being wishy-washy, though. It's about getting along well with others in a very diverse society. It's about tolerating disappointments and inconveniences. We should respond positively to the unexpected and be willing to change for the better, and we are to do it all without compromising our principles and beliefs.

Everyone should have a short list of absolutes—truths held to be self-evident, standards that demand our compliance; that should be true of us at all times. If you don't have a ready list of such precepts, then start developing one. Having inviolable precepts or a creed allows your thoughts and actions to be consistent with your beliefs and principles.

The Keffler List is rather simple to lay out, but not always easy to live by.

1. God first, family second, others third, and I'm fourth.

2. Be faithful to our religious teachings.

Granted, we'll all spend a lifetime trying to fully understand our precepts and even longer trying to live by them, but it's nice to know that everything else is negotiable. It's not unusual for one of my children to ask, "What do we believe about such and such?" Sometimes Bill and I know the answer, and sometimes we have to do some studying in order to reply intelligently. Other times we will tell our children that they can pretty much search for the truth and go where that leads them, because it's not a moral issue, doesn't involve one of the non-negotiables.

The ability to be flexible is essential in a large household. Because this is earth and not heaven, I have been blessed with what the experts call a highly sensitive child. When he was little, his shirt itched, his socks felt funny, and his shoes had to be tied about ten times before the bow would lie just right. He made me crazy. I fantasized about checking him into a monastery. The routine would accommodate his need to do everything exactly the same, day in and day out. Then I figured I'd spend all my time running over to the monastery to cut the tags out of his robe and make sure the cincture around his waist hung evenly. Besides that, he was, and is, my most consistently thoughtful child. (Maybe it's a pleasant side effect of the highly sensitive thing).

When I discovered the merits of flexibility, I decided to introduce it to my son right away. Typically, I found myself becoming more flexible about his inflexibility, which in turn, made him more flexible. It takes time, but at home and in the world at large, we have to know where to draw the line and which battles are worth fighting for.

Forgiveness

Pardoning ourselves and others for mistakes or wrongdoing without holding grudges or seeking revenge

SEEDS TO PLANT:
Forgive a friend for saying something hurtful.

WEEDS TO PULL:
Don't nurse anger.

FAMILY RULE:
Forgive and, maybe, forget.

Forgiveness is tricky. It's meant to be directed at other people but, like no other virtue, it benefits the person granting it more than it benefits the person receiving it. Yet we resist this virtue as if anger, resentment, and a desire for vengeance were treasures to be stored up.

First of all, forgiveness does not require us to withdraw or cancel consequences. Facing consequences is an important part of justice. If my daughter tells me she is sorry for misbehaving, I forgive her, but she is usually punished. To neglect to do so over anything but a minor offense would not only be an injustice, it would also mislead her in the ways of the world. Perhaps, worst of all, it could render the virtue of forgiveness meaningless. Making an apology and being forgiven would become just something you do to get the matter behind you.

People resist forgiveness because they erroneously think it requires forgetting a deed that has caused pain or other form of harm. "Forgive and forget," the saying goes. The trouble is, we withhold forgiveness because we can't forget. So we figure we will get around to forgiving when we think we are ready to forget, but that day may never come . . . and neither does the forgiveness. Besides, it isn't always prudent to forget. You can forgive a debt, but that does not require you to hand over another loan to someone who has proved untrustworthy.

Forgiveness should be granted to another person, whether or not the person who committed the wrongful act feels guilty, is repentant, or even aware of the deed. If forgiveness is a virtue, then it must be an act of will and thus we can choose to do it. Forgiveness means we let go of anger, resentment, and a desire for revenge. It is like a river: If some sort of emotional dam holds it up in us, then we will be unable to receive forgiveness from others. If we nurse anger and resentment toward others, how can we believe that others should forgive us for our wrongdoings and mistakes?

Forgiveness fosters peace of mind. A life void of a forgiving spirit is filled with bitterness. And who, besides me, suffers if I am bitter? All the people around me who had nothing to do with harming me.

Sometimes the person we have to forgive is ourselves. If we have done something we are ashamed of, we must do everything in our power to make amends. Once we have done that, we must move on with our lives. Forgetting here depends on whether the interest of everyone concerned is best served. We should not try to forget the bad results of our past indiscretions.

Forgiveness renews our lives. It helps us begin afresh, in spite of betrayal, personal agony, or even physical pain. We all know of grudges that are handed down from one generation to the next. The world would be so much better if we bequeathed to our descendants a spirit of forgiveness, instead of a spirit of getting even.

Fortitude

Having a positive attitude to overcome difficulties and resist impulses

Being courageous

SEEDS TO PLANT: Practice self-denial.

WEEDS TO PULL: Don't give in to every urge.

FAMILY RULE: Tackle your challenges bravely.

I n the opening lines of this book, I shared with you my story of fortitude and my fearful child. This cardinal virtue is my sentimental favorite, not only because it set me on a course of study about all virtues, but because it is the virtue that for me plays hard to get.

Fortitude can be dramatic, catapulting us into necessary action and holding undesirable impulses in check. When the going gets tough, it allows us to work toward making our dreams come true. Fortitude, which we may think of as inner strength or courage, demands that we do the right thing when tempted to take the easy way out.

Fortitude is not about banishing fear, but overcoming it in the pursuit of a moral life. In fact, much of what we fear is healthy and keeps us from taking unnecessary risks. To achieve a greater good, it enables us to persevere in spite of our fear. Fortitude is strong stuff and not just for slaying dragons. Sometimes, it's needed just to get out of bed in the morning to face a difficult day.

Have you ever had a fear that hung over you for the simple reason that you couldn't see into the future? You feel impending doom in your bones because of the unknown. This dread—"terror or apprehension as to something in the future; great fear," says the dictionary—has a way of acting like a sinker on our spirit. It comes upon us and takes root. Dread is what the people hiding from the Nazis must have felt. It is what a parent feels when an out-of-control teenager is on a path to self-destruction. Dread is each new day when we are grieving. It is different things to different people, but its effect can be the same—despair.

Fortitude is our rope out of the pit, the motor that keeps us moving when life is only going through the motions. It is what allows us to cling to hope. But fortitude, like other virtues, has to be developed. We have to choose to exercise it. It will only be available to us if we use it when we don't really need to. We should each day do something we ought to do but don't want to. That is why religions require fasting or other forms of self-denial, to keep us spiritually fit so we can face the worst that life has to offer and not lose heart.

No one has ever defined fortitude better than Anne Frank. What a mind this teenage girl had, and what a gift her diary is to all of us. On March 7, 1944, her entry, written when fear was an everyday companion, included this piece of wisdom: "He who has faith and courage will not perish in misery."

Friendship

An enduring relationship between two people
that is based on trust, respect, and love

SEEDS TO PLANT: Make a list of friends and plan ways to stay in touch.

WEEDS TO PULL: Don't neglect to spend time with your friends.

FAMILY RULE: Keep friends in heart and mind.

Virtuous people should try very hard to "love their neighbor," want the best for them, be helpful to them, and feel connected to them. In this sense, while genuine, it is a distant love, but it's not friendship. It springs from being in the family of mankind; it is part of the human experience.

Friendship begins in a social setting—a classroom, a front yard, a parent meeting, the workplace, a dorm room, or any situation where people spend time together and visit. If common ground is discovered during the process of becoming acquainted, then the relationship progresses. As a comfortable familiarity develops, we share more information, thoughts, opinions, and details of our lives. If the information is well received and seems to be held in confidence, then more self-disclosure takes place and trust deepens. Mutual admiration blooms.

Friends enjoy fun, light-heartedness, and camaraderie, but trust and love are what seal the bond.

The word "friendship" comes from a Germanic word meaning love and an Anglo-Saxon word meaning shape. Friendship means in the shape of love. If it looks like love and acts like love, then friendship will indeed endure like love.

We all need to develop lasting friendships. Friendships need to be mutually beneficial in that the friends make each other better persons. But in the desire to cultivate relationships, we have to be perceptive enough to avoid relationships that lead us to fall short of our moral standards. "Iron sharpens iron; so a person sharpens the countenance of a friend," says the proverb. Mutually beneficial friendship.

True friendship stands the test of time. Sometimes we are friendly with people because of a meaningful association related to a temporary common ground. But this friendly relationship may dissolve when the common ground is gone; it does not necessarily indicate failure of the relationship. But when true, lasting friendship has emerged, we need to nurture it indefinitely.

My husband, Bill, is my role model when it comes to the caring for and keeping friends. His ability to nurture long-standing friendships is an art. He has always been very deliberate about keeping in touch with notes, phone calls, and visits. He religiously keeps track of birthdays and anniversaries that are scribbled in his address book and are carefully transferred to his new appointment book every January. If that address book were legible to anyone but him, it would be an important historical document for our children's children.

In the final scene of *It's a Wonderful Life*, the angel Clarence leaves George a book signed, "Dear George, remember, no man is a failure who has friends." If taken to heart, these words should prompt us to invest as much time safeguarding our friendships as we dedicate to financial or investment planning. The reward of a life rich with friends is guaranteed.

Frugality

Using money, time, possessions, and talents
wisely and purposefully

SEEDS TO PLANT: Be orderly about spending.
WEEDS TO PULL: Don't waste time or money.
FAMILY RULE: Waste not, want not.

W hen I am short of money, I spend too much time, and when I am short of time, I spend too much money. This, in a nutshell, is my failing economic policy. Like most problems in life, if I correctly applied the right virtues, I could approach this issue more effectively.

When I'm in a hurry, my money goes to the fast-food chain, the bakery, and the fix-it man. Some weeks are so hectic that when I yell "time for dinner," the kids jump in the car. Recently, I rushed to the craft store and bought thirty dollars worth of supplies so one of my children could complete a project the night before it was due. We didn't have time to search the house for available paint, paper, and brushes. If I were more methodical, those things would have been tucked away in an art supply drawer. If my son were more orderly and had alerted me that he had a project, I wouldn't have been at the grocery store at 9 P.M. buying celery and food coloring for a science experiment. Of course, while I was there I picked up prepackaged lunches because I didn't want to be making sandwiches at midnight after we cleared away the project. Too much money is spent putting out fires, and not enough of our time is spent planning.

Frugality—never to be confused with being miserly or stingy—would make for more peaceful living in all areas of life. It needs to become a habit, because we would be less likely to be short of money if we always were frugal with it. I once read that very wealthy people tend to be very thrifty about household items and daily expenses. For me, money flies out the window when I have not taken the time to plan menus or shop in advance for birthdays or holidays.

Frugality stops waste in its tracks. It means the right amount of time and money is spent on everything on a regular basis. When we are frugal with our possessions, they are properly taken care of and last longer. This virtue enables us to use our talents wisely, which in turn enriches our lives and the lives of others.

We are responsible for using our talents and gifts well. Not to do so is ingratitude. I heard a clergyman say that he received a guitar from his brother-in-law and put it under his bed for several years because he didn't have the money for lessons. Late in his teens he took it out and started to play around with it. He was stunned to discover he could play it by ear. Now he uses it constantly in his work, and other people,

particularly young people, can enjoy his talent. He apologized to his brother-in-law for waiting so long to show his gratitude by using the gift he had been given. The gift of the guitar allowed him to use another gift he didn't even know he had.

My grandfather used to say, "You measure success not by how much you earn, but by how much you save." Being frugal in all areas allows you to spend your gifts and talents lavishly.

Generosity

Sharing your time, talent, and possessions with others

Understanding what you have to offer

SEEDS TO PLANT: Give others the benefit of the doubt.

WEEDS TO PULL: Don't entertain critical thoughts toward others.

FAMILY RULE: Give thanks and share.

Maximilian Kolbe, a Catholic priest, lived near Warsaw. A few weeks after the Nazis invaded Poland in 1939, he was arrested; eventually he was sent to Auschwitz, a concentration, or death, camp. Ten people were sentenced to the starvation bunker because one man had escaped. Father Kolbe stepped forward to change places with one of the ten, who was a husband and father.

Very few of us will ever be in a position to be so completely generous, but every day we are presented many opportunities to practice this gentle virtue.

Once a year, in December, we all switch to a generous mode. I think this sincere generosity is reflected on people's faces. Contrary to widespread opinion, I believe their spirit of generosity, not the gift-giving, is what accounts for the happy attitudes during the holidays. It feels so good to be generous. The many greeting cards we receive ought to motivate us to keep the spirit of the holidays throughout the year. Most of us intend to, but we forget, perhaps because the general atmosphere disappears with the festive decorations of the season. No one is standing on the street corner ringing a little bell, calling us to service. I know one mother who keeps a small bell in her kitchen for just this purpose. It's to remind her children to be generous;

she uses it when she hears unkind words or demanding tones. When her children hear the bell, they are reminded to rephrase their statement or change their tone.

When we practice the virtue of generosity, a spirit of being liberal in sharing our possessions and our self, we see people in the best possible light. How often is our day ruined because of the defensive or critical response we make to the way other people behave? One time, during a planning meeting for a charity event, I was totally aggravated with the impatient attitude and demeanor of a committee member. We were all under pressure to meet deadlines, so I found myself snapping back. How ironic that we were all there to do "good work," but we were at each other's throats.

A few days later, I learned that the other person's father had become gravely ill. Was I ever ashamed! I should have given her the benefit of the doubt. If my attitude had been more generous, I would have treated her more like I usually did. Even if she was just having a bad day, giving her the benefit of the doubt would have cost me nothing. Being the demeanor monitor is hard work and not recommended.

Understanding that we can have a good effect on others is a basis for our generosity. After all, how can we be open-handed with our possessions or ourselves if we don't recognize that we have something to offer them? It's heartening to look around and think, "Hey, I can make a difference here." When you work at having a generous spirit, people will be attracted to you and that is a good thing, because part of being generous is being inclusive.

We should look for ways to include others. Eye contact and a smile for someone you pass on the street is one small example of generosity. This may be especially meaningful to the homeless person, a disabled person, or to the grumpy neighbor down the street. For a tiny moment, they will experience the warm feeling of being included. These small efforts aren't much compared to the heroic gesture of Maximilian Kolbe, but it is generous, and because it is a beacon of light in a dark world.

Gratitude

Being grateful for your blessings, talents, and friends

Expressing your appreciation to others

SEEDS TO PLANT: Count your blessings.

WEEDS TO PULL: No crying until . . .

FAMILY RULE: Be thankful and content.

G ratitude is a perspective of life that enables you to be content with what you have, avoid envy of what others have, and withstand hardship. It is an attitude to be cultivated, recognizing what we owe to others. Even during the worst moments of life, the sun still rises and the birds still sing. We all have times that are difficult, but with gratitude we can maintain a positive attitude and enjoy a panoramic view of life.

Suzanne Etman, my friend, partner, and illustrator, grew up in a large home. Parents of any size family get tired of whining and crying, but when the number of children goes up, the tolerance for tears goes down.

When Suzanne's loving but firm father, Dee, saw a tearful child, he said, "No crying until you get hit by a train." It was his way of reminding the kids to be grateful for what they had and not whine about what they didn't have or cry about things not going their way. Crying was for serious things, like being hit by a train, something that almost never happens.

Mary, Suzanne's mother, loves to reminisce about the time that Danny, one of Suzanne's little brothers, born with cerebral palsy, along with younger brother Matthew, decided to take a 300-mile trip to San Antonio to visit a little boy Danny met during a hospital stay. The police had found them on the highway. Four-year-old Matthew was pushing eight-year-old Danny in his wheelchair. George, the family dog, was tied to the side of the chair and appeared to be a willing accomplice.

A few years ago, Suzanne's father called all the children home. "We have been hit by a train," he told them with tear-filled eyes. Danny had died. His cerebral palsy had presented the family with difficult challenges, but they didn't view his life as tragic. They cherish the memories of him and are grateful for the joy he brought into their lives.

Disregarding your blessings because times are trying robs you of the simple pleasures that abound. The trick is to recognize them. How inclined we are to concentrate on what we don't have and be blind to source of the gifts we do have. After all, what do we have that we have not received? When a problem hovers over us or the specter of envy dances around us, we become forgetful of the blessings that are ours, and to that extent ungrateful.

Gratitude sheds light on our perspective and allows us to recognize a train when we see one, and not waste tears on anything else.

Hospitality

Creating in your home an ongoing atmosphere
of warmth and welcome toward family
and visitors alike

SEEDS TO PLANT:
Make guests feel like family.

WEEDS TO PULL:
Don't save your best for guests.

FAMILY RULE:
Make your home a haven.

We recognize that host, hospital, hotel, hospice, hostel, hostile, and hospitality all appear to be related words, with common roots. Our interest here is hospitality, which long ago may have meant providing life-giving care for strangers in dire need of water, food, and shelter. A person who owned a dwelling, we might say, felt an obligation to host strangers in their hostels because times were hostile.

Our home, in hostile times or not, is to be a haven for our family, friends, and, when prudent, strangers. Family living requires that our home appeal to a wide range of people. This is rather challenging at my house because we have five rambunctious children, two equally rambunctious dogs, and usually an assortment of high-spirited young friends.

I have an ongoing fantasy of inviting a friend in and having her leave her worries at the door because of the tranquil setting of my home. It is more likely that she will get knocked over by the kids, if not by one of the dogs. An adult will be inclined to edge into my house the way a cautious driver maneuvers around a dangerous curve. My house is never going to have a "House Beautiful" feel to it, but what really matters is the warmth and graciousness the guest—old friend, relative, exchange student, business associate—finds there. People enjoy coming to a house where it seems like you have been just waiting for them to show up.

That's the way Bill's mom reflected hospitality. When Bill and I were about to get engaged, I started hearing from his hometown friends, "Just wait till you meet Bill's mother." "You are going to have a dream-come-true mother-in-law." Bill has two brothers, and it seemed that Ruth Keffler couldn't wait for one of her boys to get married so that there would be another female in the family. She was convinced that girls should be treated special.

The first morning I was in her guest room, she brought me coffee on a tray. I looked at her, thanked her, and then laughed. "Ruth, I'm one of six children. The only time a tray has been brought to me in bed was when I was in isolation because I had something contagious." From there we moved to the breakfast room and sat chatting at the table for hours, which in time became a ritual.

Ruth had a way of making you feel you were the most interesting person she had ever known. Bill said she was always like that, When he was little, he had to drag his friends out of the kitchen so they could go play.

Our children loved sitting at Grandma's table. They would draw, play Go Fish, and watch the birds outside the large window near the table. A bird feeder, always crowded with birds, was often the subject of pictures and conversation. Even the birds liked making themselves at home with Ruth. She would spend hours telling the kids stories about her three sons when they were younger. It occurred to me that one of the reasons why Ruth visited so well with people was that her attentiveness to them helped her to get to really know them.

Like most truly gracious people, Ruth reserved her best hospitality for her family. She figured if your own children like being at home, their friends would like it too.

Humility

Knowing your strengths and weaknesses, respecting authority

Accepting and treating others as equals

SEEDS TO PLANT: Keep a list of your strengths and weaknesses.

WEEDS TO PULL: Don't forget to read the directions.

FAMILY RULE: Look for the best in yourself and others.

H umility is the foundation of all the virtues: therefore, in a soul where it does not exist, there can be no true virtue, but the mere appearance only," wrote Saint Augustine. It has also been called the elusive virtue because once you think you possess it, you've lost it. So how do you go about developing this foundation of all other virtues, and at the same time, avoid feeling that you possess it so you don't lose it all over again?

"Know yourself" is an ancient Greek adage. Humility must be rooted in truth. We must be realistic and honest about ourselves, acknowledging our strengths and our weaknesses. We should see our talents as gifts to be shared, willing to use them in service to others. We should also try to overcome, or at least compensate for, our weaknesses. It's no accident that "humble" and "human" are closely related words.

A truly humble person expects more of self than others, but is quick to praise others. We can't be stingy with compliments and praise for the people around us. Children resist complimenting other children. They seem to think that granting plaudits to playmates or teammates gives the other guys an advantage. I tell my little athletes that lauding a friend's pitching or running helps keep competition friendly and helps them avoid pride.

Humility ensures that we accept and treat others as equals. Their needs and wants are just as important as our own. If everyone in the world embraced humility, we could eradicate bigotry and prejudice entirely. No one else's life is more or less valuable than our own.

We can practice humility consistently in the course of daily living. Cutting in front of other drivers in traffic implies that my schedule is more urgent, my time more valuable, than theirs. Getting up and walking out of McDonald's without clearing your table indicates that other people should clean up your mess. I tell my kids that even if they become the president of the United States, no one should have to pick up their dirty socks and underwear.

Humility helps us avoid what I call the "I didn't think it could happen to me" syndrome. I remember reading an interview in 1969 with Helen Hayes,

First Lady of the American Theater. Her words have stayed with me for thirty years. She was talking about her daughter's death from polio years earlier. Miss Hayes said losing her daughter was devastating, but her grief healed. Her husband never stopped grieving because he never stopped asking "Why me?" On the other hand, she saw that the disease was ravaging thousands of lives. Her response was "Why not me?" It didn't occur to her that her family should be spared.

The "Why me?" and the "Why not me?" comments are reasonable questions to ask ourselves in the pursuit of humility, but not in the way we normally ask them. When it comes to our blessings, we should ask "Why me?" When it comes to the crosses that we bear, we should ask "Why not me?" These two questions should help us become humble. Our answers to these questions should help us stay that way.

Individuality

The qualities, talents, and personality
that make each person
unique in all the world

SEEDS TO PLANT: Find a way to express your individuality.

WEEDS TO PULL: Don't copy.

FAMILY RULE: Be true to yourself.

This book contains fifty-three of the numberless virtues found in various writings, including sacred texts. If every person in one town embraced these fifty-three virtues with the same intensity, no two people would seem any more alike than they do now. It would be a very pleasant town in which to reside—and it wouldn't be boring or even seem uniform. Individuality cannot be stamped out, but it can be misunderstood and underappreciated. To be a virtue, it must have a moral purpose.

The first step in developing individuality relies heavily on humility. You have to know who you are and what you have to offer. Individuality means that a methodical person appreciates his abilities to maintain order, but is happy that his artistic friend is around to bring some color and beauty to the banquet of life.

My oldest son, Joe, lives, eats, breathes, and sleeps sports. He has his whole life planned and everything is related to his love of the game—any game. I enjoy watching him and all my children play sports, but I don't have a deep affection for athletics. Still, about three times a week I take the trouble to listen to a sports talk show. Occasionally, I'm able to dazzle my Joe with details or a unique insight to some sports-related event.

Of course, I told him where I was getting my information. He was surprised that I listened and, when he found out why, he was touched. My interest, or lack thereof, in sports is immaterial. Anything that interests him interests me because of my interest in him. I learned this from my father who always found a way to connect with all six of his children.

As kids, we were not spoiled with material things. If we developed a sincere interest in something, though, my parents gave us every opportunity to explore that interest. One of my sisters and I loved horses. We lived in the country on a lake and were able to have horses. Now my sister and her husband own a small ranch. When my brothers developed a persistent interest in water skiing, my parents invested in a modest boat. They encouraged us to learn everything we could about our interests and hobbies and when we were older they helped us locate jobs that were related to our interests.

Obviously, my father was not personally interested in everything we were, but his enthusiasm for and interest in what we were doing encouraged us. He appreciated the fact that we were not interested in the same things. He didn't seem to value any one thing over another. This did wonders for our individuality. Competition was not an issue.

When you're the parents of five children, this appreciation of their individuality—their uniqueness—results in a lot of wear and tear on your schedules as well as your car. It helped us help our children find niches in which they could at least try to excel. Individuality helps people refine their humility; celebrating it helps them rise to their full potential.

Industriousness

Working dutifully,
diligently, and lovingly

Encouraging others to do the same

SEEDS TO PLANT: Do things the right way.

WEEDS TO PULL: Don't feel burdened with activities.

FAMILY RULE   Love what you do.

We have job-related work and life-related work. We need to have the self-discipline to get things done, avoid laziness, and inspire others to join us in useful and productive activities. We should always leave time for recreation, contemplation, socializing, and worship, but idleness is the devil's playground. Life is fulfilling when there is some point to what we are doing, an awareness that in fact we have achieved something worthwhile.

Children's work is playing. While they should have household duties and school work, they should be allowed to play. Activities that require imagination and creativity are how they work at playing. Toys that do all the work spoil the fun more than children, or parents, realize. But being busy just for its own sake robs work of its deepest meaning.

Watching too much television fools us into thinking we are just filling a time slot. It can keep us from recognizing boredom which is usually a condition that motivates us to get busy and do something interesting or enriching. Reading a good book also fills time, but it's an activity that is much more likely than television to inspire us or elevate our thinking.

Doing worthwhile work is not all that's required of us if we are to be industrious. We should strive to do the work to the best of our ability and, if need be, learn to do it better. The desire to do things in the best way possible enhances the value of our work, as well as of our recreational activities and hobbies. The industrious person wants to see progress and the desired results in what he or she is doing.

We all know the story of Tom Sawyer painting the fence and making it look like fun so his friends would offer to do it for him. His intentions were not noble, but the principle there is reasonable. When we take pleasure in doing things well, we inspire the people around us. They, too, will want to experience the rewards of industriousness.

As for most virtues, the underlying motive for being industrious is love, for ourselves and others. We should be industrious because we need and enjoy the fruits of our labor. Work, far from being viewed as drudgery, should be seen as the dignified activity by which we fulfill our needs and express the human desire to create.

Integrity

Being consistently honorable in thought, word, and deed

SEEDS TO PLANT: Pay the full fare.

WEEDS TO PULL: Don't "borrow" from the workplace.

FAMILY RULE: Life is not fair, so get over it.

*U*nderstanding the difference between fairness and integrity is a great step forward in acquiring the habit of integrity.

The sign says "Six and Under Eat Free." You are standing there with your seven-year-old son who just celebrated his birthday the week before. You begin to rationalize:

"This time last week he was six." "My seven-year-old eats more like a six-year-old." "The prices are too high anyway." You decide to right this wrong by passing him off as six years old. So, in addition to breaching integrity, you have given your child a crash course in rationalization—the enemy of integrity. Is this worth the five dollars you saved?

The bottom line is this: If you do not think the price is fair, eat somewhere else. A proprietor gets to decide what to charge for the food. The consumer gets to decide how much to spend. Integrity is not served when we run around policing fairness. Fairness is subjective. Integrity is objective.

An eight-year-old does not think it's fair that his twelve-year-old brother gets to stay up an hour later. Now ask the eight-year-old if it's fair for him to stay up a half-hour later than his five-year-old sister. The objective parent recognizes what is the appropriate bedtime for each child. Generally speaking, we all tend to be overly concerned about unfairness when our own interests and desires are at stake.

Our friends, the Bonnets, feel so strongly about their children comprehending this fact that their family motto is "Life is not fair, so get over it." They say it with a smile, of course. Their point is that time spent fighting over "unfairness" is better spent pursuing integrity.

Other chinks in the armor of integrity include taking home supplies from the office, keeping the money when we are given too much change at the store, and cheating on income tax. Typical rationalizations for these actions are: "I put in lots of overtime." "It's not my mistake." "It's my money and I earned it."

People of integrity are honorable because they are high-minded in thought, speak truthfully, and do the right thing. People of principle do not waste time rationalizing, and others can count on their honesty. They do what is right in every situation because they are more concerned with having integrity—being honorable, moral, conscientious—than in being treated fairly.

Jocularity

Spending time having fun, being playful,
and participating in light-hearted diversions

SEEDS TO PLANT: Lighten up.

WEEDS TO PULL: Don't outlaw roughhousing.

FAMILY RULE: Take time out for fun.

L ife is serious business, but probably not as serious as most of us make it. Jocularity is a "mental health" virtue that helps us take the breaks from our cares and concerns that we all deserve. Jocularity is time out for just plain fun, a time to unwind. Planned recreation such as golf, tennis, or fishing can be very intense and even stressful, but jocularity de-stresses our lives. Some people are snared in the work trap: everything they do, they do as work, even supposedly recreational, fun activities. This mentality is to be avoided.

A little roughhousing is permitted and even encouraged at my house. It's more fun to wrestle Dad in the family room than out in the yard. You have to have furniture to hide behind if you're going to have a sock war. Balled-up socks also come in handy when whacked with rolled newspaper bats. And you can't run to the bases on your knees when you play baseball at the park. Roughhousing is a good exercise and not nearly as boring as jogging on your own.

One father I know took his five kids and two of mine who were spending the night to a field behind his house for a midnight game of Frisbee. Bill regularly lets each of our kids bring a friend and they all play hide and seek at his office after it gets dark. One of Rebecca's fondest memories is playing "hide the baby." Her Dad would hide the youngest member of her family and all the other kids would look for her.

Jocularity can be physical but it does not have to be. Help your kids pull off a midnight raid of the refrigerator by stocking it with the supplies needed for ice cream sundaes. Give them a hint by telling them ice cream tastes the very best at midnight. You might even leave them a note asking them to wake you so you can join the fun.

Harmless practical jokes are another way to encourage jocularity. Helping your youngest child short-sheet your oldest child's bed gives the youngest child a delicious moment of triumph. It gives the oldest child a chance to be generous. My youngest daughter loves to scare me by putting a fake roach where she'll hear me scream when I come upon it.

It has been said that a family that prays together, stays together. I think it can also be said that a family that plays together, stays together.

Joyfulness

Having a deep sense of well-being that comes from love

SEEDS TO PLANT: Choose love every chance you get.

WEEDS TO PULL: Don't isolate yourself from others.

FAMILY RULE: Love!

S uffering is underrated and not the source of misery we believe it to be. It comes to us physically and emotionally, but if we are joyful, it will not come to us spiritually. Spiritual suffering, the result of decisions we make, is the only suffering that can make us despair.

Leprosy affects the peripheral nervous system and destroys sensation. People infected by leprosy have no sense of touch and cannot feel pain by contact. They can hurt themselves unknowingly as infection sets in and it's not realized until it's too late. A particle in the eye, because they don't feel it, can eventually result in serious damage. If we don't feel pain, we can't fix what's wrong. If we can't feel pain in our hand, we won't feel the hot stove top, and we also can't draw warmth from another person's touch.

The only way we can be assured of avoiding emotional pain is by avoiding contact with other people. No rational person would inoculate themselves against pain and suffering if they realized they were, at the same time, relinquishing the ability to give and receive love.

The spiritual person inside each of us knows that we are created for love, and all the pain, suffering, and sacrifice in life cannot suppress the joy derived from this gift. Joy is, as a Roman philosopher noted, an "impregnable fortress." The virtue of joyfulness is learned, and the teachers are pain and suffering. The enduring sense of well-being that comes from it is based on the conviction that, with love, all will be well. Joyfulness shines the brightest in the darkest moments of life.

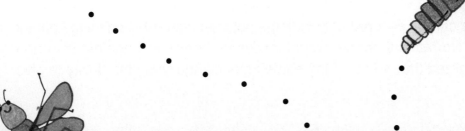

Justice

Being righteous in all things

Behaving honorably toward others and expecting others to behave honorably toward you

Accepting the consequences of your actions

SEEDS TO PLANT: Play by the rules.

WEEDS TO PULL: Don't be prejudiced.

FAMILY RULE: Treat others the way you want to be treated.

Almost everything I've read on justice defines it as giving other people their due. Okay, but what does this mean? What are they due? Who is in charge of making sure everyone has his or her due? Ultimately, we all have a role in seeing that everyone gets what she or he is rightfully owed. The purpose of social order is to ensure "justice for all," as the Pledge of Allegiance expresses it.

The conviction that there are acts that are right and some that are wrong is a prerequisite to forming an opinion about what is specifically right or wrong in regard to self, to others, and to society. The notion of justice may seem vague or obscure when we consider the fact that free will and a free country mean that there will not necessarily be agreement on what is right behavior and what is wrong.

We have to have a well-formed conscience and strong conviction about right and wrong. If we see something is morally wrong but not illegal, we have to tolerate people's right to do it. If we are morally outraged, then we have an obligation to try to change minds and seek to change laws in peaceful, legal ways.

It's helpful to remember that prudence helps us judge whether an action is right or wrong. A sense of justice guides us in determining what we should do about it. Being determined to make justice a continuing part of our lives, in all our relationships and in our dealings with institutions, requires ongoing righteous action in matters large and small. Personal justice is relentlessly honest because it is revealed more in what we do than in what we say. Since we are not perfect and fall short of constant right action, we must hold ourselves personally accountable for our misdeeds by accepting all the consequences.

Since justice is revealed in our actions, no wonder the universally accepted ideal for justice, the Golden Rule, describes our moral outlook: "Do unto others as you would have them do to you." This is the simple but challenging prescription for justice. Living this way, day in and day out, educates your children in ways that words alone cannot.

Kindness

Giving preference to the needs and feelings of others

SEEDS TO PLANT:
Place others before yourself.

WEEDS TO PULL:
Don't take family for granted.

FAMILY RULE:
If you can't say something nice,
don't say anything at all.

R emember the Avis commercial about trying harder because in the car rental business they were the number two behind Hertz? Showing kindness is all about being number two. Putting other people first makes life more gentle and bearable, and it is one form of instant gratification that is virtuous.

Fulton Sheen said, "Courtesy is kindness without parade of favors; it is tender and affectionate in looks and acts, always giving preference to others in every little enjoyment." If you are familiar with the Random Acts of Kindness movement, then you are aware of the appeal of this altruistic virtue.

Being kind to strangers is a short-term commitment. Letting the other guy have the parking spot, being friendly to the sanitation worker, and offering the plumber a glass of iced tea are small acts of kindness that make the world a nicer place and give you a charge. Being kind every time the opportunity presents itself helps to form a solid habit. Long-term gratification arises when the habit of kindness is rooted in home life.

Kindness toward family members makes our homes loving retreats. Hard knocks received on the school and work fronts can be disheartening, but to know we can come home and receive consolation makes the disapproval and rejection we receive elsewhere bearable.

Arguments and fussing are a part of family life, but one of our firmest household rules is that disagreements must be settled without yelling, name calling, or hitting. When you outlaw those three things, about the only thing left is peaceful arbitration and negotiation. Hostility and bitterness can't take root in such an atmosphere.

This attitude, though tested occasionally, paid off when one of my children suffered challenging times in middle school. I resisted the temptation to call mothers and teachers, since I'm sure my child was not exclusively on the receiving end of mean-spiritedness. The bottom line was that she would have to work through it on her own. Meanwhile, my husband and I tried to put a lot of emphasis on having fun at home as a family. As a result, invitations and phone calls that weren't forthcoming were not missed as much and we all became closer.

When I see irreverent, cocky adolescents, it breaks my heart. The problem obviously isn't always a poor home situation, but the rougher the kids appear, the emptier they seem. Gangs are about acceptance and belonging. We have counseled our children that they may not drive one another away with hatefulness or belittling behavior. Nothing warms our heart more than to see them, with simple kindness, support one another, sacrifice for and back one another up, and put the other first by guarding their hearts from criticism and meanness.

Loyalty

Being faithful to family, friends, community, and country

Being steadfast in your religious and ethical beliefs

SEEDS TO PLANT: Family first.

WEEDS TO PULL: Never speak ill of family members.

FAMILY RULE: Our family sticks together.

When I was growing up in a household of six children, there were plenty of lively quarrels. My mother, for the most part, would stay out of the line of fire. She would frequently say, "Bicker all you want here, but you'd better stick up for one another outside this house."

We must have taken her words to heart because everyone in the neighborhood knew that if you took on one Bondurant, you had to take on all of them.

When I was in the first grade I followed my sister Terrie around during recess. She was in the third grade. Sister Mary Joseph told Terrie that she was to insist I find playmates from the first grade. Terrie looked at Sister and told her respectfully but firmly that I could be with her as much as I wanted. "Sister, Mom says we can fight all we want at home but everywhere else we stick together." Sister was amused and impressed.

"Honor your mother and father" is a commandment that children grasp at an early age. Not only does it insist on obedience, it teaches us to hold in high esteem what our parents hold in high esteem. The first notion of

Loyalty is learned in the home. We think important what our parents think is important. My parents spoke in the third person: "Bondurants don't lie." "Bondurants are polite." "Bondurants aren't quitters." Eventually, a code of family honor evolved in each one of us. This created in us a great sense of family pride and self-possession that gave us something to live up to and fall back on.

Once family honor is established, the virtue of loyalty extends almost naturally to every area of our life. Loyalty to friends, community, country, and religious beliefs becomes tied up in our identity. It also, ironically, facilitates independence. When people know who they are and what they stand for, peer pressure, drugs, and promiscuity hold little attraction.

As adults, my brothers and sisters and I have discussed what our parents did to firmly instill in us the family code of honor. While we have plenty of foibles and are by no means perfect people, we have never strayed from the fold. We have arrived at several unwritten precepts that my parents consistently reinforced. We are all trying to duplicate these qualities in our own homes.

Those precepts are: (1) Home was the center of their lives. Neither Mom nor Dad had compelling outside interests. Hobbies were pursued within the family. (2) Dinner was at 6:00 P.M. every night and everyone was expected to be at the table. (3) Friends, boyfriends, and girlfriends were always welcome to join our family gathering, but we could not be away from the house two nights in a row. (4) Missing curfew was avoided at all costs. Not calling if we were going to be late was unthinkable. (5) Church attendance every Sunday was a given. (6) And never, under any circumstances, ride a motorcycle, . . . but we won't get into that.

Mirthfulness

Developing a sense of humor
that is tasteful and appropriate

Learning to laugh with others
and at yourself

SEEDS TO PLANT: Read the comics.

WEEDS TO PULL: Don't take yourself too seriously.

FAMILY RULE: Laugh every chance you get.

There is nothing like laughter to help keep a proper perspective on life. The ability to laugh is one of the qualities we humans possess that separates us from all the other animals on the planet. We should work as hard at developing a sense of humor as we do any other ability or gift.

Mary Linn is a friend of the family who has what I describe as a contagious laugh. No matter how bad my day has been, if I spend fifteen minutes with her I can suddenly laugh at myself and see the comedic aspects of what I previously considered a series of disasters.

The ability to laugh at oneself is disarming. If children can learn to laugh at themselves at an early age, the teasing and ribbing they receive at school will roll off their backs and they will be appreciated for their sense of humor—even before they or their classmates know there is such a thing.

There is a thin line between cruel teasing and lighthearted teasing. Teasing experienced in a friendly way at home can help children take and deliver a tease in a way that is not mean-spirited. To taunt anyone in an area that is personally sensitive is inappropriate and wrong.

Another example of inappropriate humor is tasteless jokes that are vulgar or unchaste. And under no circumstances should we participate in or encourage jokes that defame other races or cultures. People may laugh at them but it is usually an uncomfortable or squeamish laugh. Ideally, we should have the courage to point out the injustice in jokes such as these. We should never perpetuate them by retelling them. Humor should enhance life, not degrade it; provide insight into human nature, not ridicule it.

Laughter is the best medicine. Norman Cousins, former editor of *The Saturday Review,* proved it when he became critically ill. He used laughter to help fight his disease. He watched funny movies and read humorous stories and wrote a book about it called *Head First: The Biology of Hope.* When I'm overwhelmed by my child-rearing responsibilities, one of my favorite shows is Bill Cosby's *By Myself.* Or I read a book or article by someone like Erma

Bombeck. Laughter comes easily and I'm able to see the humor in what I do on a day-to-day basis.

"A good laugh is sunshine in a house," William Makepeace Thackeray, the English novelist who specialized in brilliant satire, pointed out. He didn't become famous or successful until his young wife became very ill and he needed money for her care and for raising their two daughters. Perhaps he appreciated the necessity of mirthfulness amid such family trauma.

Modesty

Being careful about what you say and do

Respecting your privacy and the privacy of others

Using good manners so you don't offend others

SEEDS TO PLANT: Keep family matters private.

WEEDS TO PULL: Don't gossip.

FAMILY RULE: Never ridicule or embarrass others.

Modesty is not about being prim and proper or blushing. Neither is it a polite way of describing someone's financial circumstances. Modesty, which is a form of moderation, is a wonderful virtue that values decency of speech, behavior, and dress. It allows us to have a sense of propriety and discretion, practice self-control, and be considerate of other people's feelings. There is a right time for everything we do and say. A firm grasp of modesty allows us to be prudent about how we act around other people and about the kind of information we share.

One thing families can do to encourage a modest comportment is to establish their own standard for dress, language, and demeanor. Adolescents understandably get very caught up with "fitting in." I don't expect my children to be the standard bearers of propriety and deportment, but I do expect them to dress appropriately in terms of time, place, and age.

Once I heard through the ever-dependable grapevine that one of my sons was using bad language. I let him know I had heard exactly what he said. He blushed, but added, "Mom, all the guys talk that way." I resisted the temptation to talk about jumping off cliffs and told him that people, even eleven-year-old boys, don't notice when you don't use bad language. They do notice when you do, and you run the risk of offending people. "Good point," he said. Sometimes you skip the lecture and help them find an out that allows them to save face with their peers.

"Hold your fork right" was a frequently heard admonishment my father made at dinner. We tried to tell him that his preoccupation with the rules of etiquette was shallow and elitist. He said, "But at least you won't embarrass yourself, or me, if you are having dinner at the White House." He was right, and while I have not eaten dinner at the White House, knowing which fork to use has given me confidence on numerous occasions.

What do proper manners have to do with virtue? As I matured, I realized the purpose of good manners is to show respect for other people. I was in a wedding shortly after graduation from college where the mother of the bride used protocol like a weapon. If any of us made the slightest mistake, she looked down her nose at us. If we are using the rules of decorum to make other people feel inadequate, then we are not being virtuous.

Learning to be careful about what we say and do, when and with whom, sounds archaic in view of the current support-group mentality when being honest is so healthy. I maintain that we should be very prudent about how much "sharing" we do. Sometimes we tell people things that no one has any business knowing. It's not dishonest to keep private matters private.

I have been guilty of sharing information about one friend to another and calling it "concern." But no matter what I called it, it was still gossip. Plain and simple. I know I have to be cautious in my speech because the lives of others often seem so much more interesting than mine.

Optimism

Having confidence in your ability to cope
with difficult challenges

Assessing situations realistically, having faith that
good will prevail

SEEDS TO PLANT: Look for the best in others.

WEEDS TO PULL: Avoid wishful thinking.

FAMILY RULE: Accentuate the positive.

I used to think that I was a natural optimist because I believed everything would turn out all right if I really believed it would. Wrong. The first time things didn't go my way, I embraced a kind of alternative optimism; Pollyanna called it the "glad game." When you are faced with a disappointment, reflect on how it could have been worse and be glad it wasn't. While accentuating the positive is a part of optimism, it stops short of this virtue because it is too passive. Optimism is far more powerful.

Optimistic people see things clearly. When we can assess situations accurately, it is easier to form an appropriate response. Ignoring certain facts in a tough situation only hinders our ability to find the best solution.

To keep optimistic fires burning, we should keep in mind that there are experts to consult and we should seek their help if it is needed. Where, after all, can you find a totally unique problem? One of the things we do to encourage our children in optimism is to make sure they spend time with a variety of trustworthy adults. Rebecca's husband Rick has shown my kids the intricacies of programming our VCR. Another friend, Steve, who is an athletic director and a math teacher, helped one of my sons with his hook shot and tutored my daughter in algebra. Recently, another friend, Tom, observed one of my sons at football practice. He sent us an e-mail praising Joe's ability and his attitude, which we in turn showed to Joe. This unsolicited, positive feedback reinforced my son's efforts. Our children know they can count on other adults to be there for them.

We can also maintain optimism if we make a habit of using our gifts and talents. Looking for ways to be purposeful keeps us moving in a positive direction. The sense of being needed is galvanizing, but we must make ourselves available to help others.

One of the most enlightening things I heard in the aftermath of the shootings at Columbine High School in Colorado is that youngsters (and all of us) need to be constantly reminded that life is a journey. We will all experience both sadness and happiness and everything in between on this journey. Optimism helps us tolerate disappointments and even tragedy, because these are not permanent conditions unless we let them be. New beginnings are there for the taking. When we choose to make a fresh start, our confidence is boosted by what we learned in the school of hard knocks.

How do you bolster optimism in the face of tragedy such as a terminal illness or a crisis that can't be resolved in the foreseeable future? Optimism is not insurance against pain and suffering, but it helps us get through them. I believe that distress in all its forms can teach us valuable lessons and help make life more meaningful. Near the end of his book *Man's Search For Meaning*, Nazi death camp survivor Victor E. Frankl wrote, "The world is in a bad state, but everything will become still worse unless each of us does his best." This is what the virtue of optimism helps us do.

Orderliness

Managing time, people, places, and things wisely
in order to pursue more worthwhile goals

Understanding that there is a natural order to life

SEEDS TO PLANT: Have something to look forward to.

WEEDS TO PULL: Don't overcommit yourself.

FAMILY RULE: Find a place for everything, and put everything in its place.

I require a minimum standard of orderliness in our house. There is a place for everything and sooner or later everything ends up in or near its place. We are dependent on routines, because they are effective and kids can learn and follow them when they are simple. When household activities such as cooking, cleaning, doing laundry, coming and going are performed on a routine basis, things go more smoothly and in a less time-consuming manner. Harmony reigns in the physical and practical concerns of our home when we are deliberate about our routines.

Harmony in the laundry room doesn't mean very much if the individual lives of family members are in disarray. You wouldn't let your child ride her bike to a neighbor's house if she had not already learned to look both ways when crossing the street. Ten year olds at R-rated movies, sexually active teenagers, underage drinking, and parents supplying hotel rooms for prom night are among the practices that disregard the natural order.

"You have to have something to look forward to" was my mother's favorite line. Any time we wanted to do something that she thought we were too young to do, those words followed a firm "No." It was what she told me when I wanted to wear mascara when I was in the seventh grade. Lipstick at twelve. A little blush at thirteen. Mascara at fourteen. I could not understand then why it was okay for my lashes to look longer and thicker in ninth grade but not in seventh grade. The older my children get, the better I understand her thinking and it has become a frequent response of mine. It seems I've joined my mother's club.

Children are growing up much too fast. We seem to have lost all sense of order in the maturing process. Our culture is intrusive. Billboards alone can increase the libidinal age by three years between any five exits on I-35 in Dallas, Texas. Throw in graphic news headlines from our nation's capital, provocative music, sexually explicit television programs, and before you know it your twelve-year-old is thinking like a twenty-one-year-old with questionable moral judgment.

Parents think they can't override the influence of the culture. Maybe they submit to it out of apathy or ignorance or fatigue. Sometimes they just lack the fortitude to confront their kids. A great activity for any family is to make a list of privileges and then assign reasonable ages at which children may expect to do them. Explain to your children the common sense behind your thinking; invite them to join the "You Have to Have Something to Look Forward to" club.

There is also a need for interpersonal orderliness. If you hurt someone, you tell the person you're sorry. If you break something, you get it repaired or replace it. If one family member needs a little extra attention, other family members should try to offer it. If one child has a problem, others in the family should make themselves available to help with a solution.

Orderliness brings harmony to all the nuances of family living. When we respect the natural order of things, we avoid problems and life is more peaceful. Abiding by a priority—"first things first"—allows us be proactive instead of reactive. We must teach our children this skill so that they will understand homework before play, marriage before sex, maturity before marriage, and, naturally, mascara before all of the above (except for homework).

Patience

Being calm in spite of uncertainty, aggravation, difficulty, and plain boredom

SEEDS TO PLANT: Speak in a calm tone.

WEEDS TO PULL: Don't buy on impulse.

FAMILY RULE: Listen quietly while others are talking.

O n the surface, patience seems to be something we are either born with or without, like having perfect pitch or being tone deaf. If patience is a virtue, as the saying goes, then it can be learned. Patience is getting where you want to go and making the ride as pleasant as possible. It's needed with everyone, but perhaps most of all with ourselves.

A missing shoe, a traffic jam, and a slow store clerk are all good opportunities to practice patience. Situations like these that try our patience are inconveniences, not full-blown crises. Yet by being guarded about our attitude and conduct we can train ourselves to respond in a way that is measured and calm.

Being patient is the willingness to take the steps necessary to achieve a worthwhile end. It usually means doing things with a lot more effort, so they are done once and for all. Anyone who has potty trained a toddler knows that a two-year-old will want to tour every public restroom he can find for a few weeks after he is in big boy pants. So at the mall you shift packages and search out the nearest bathroom only to hear,

"I guess I don't need to go." Replayed often enough, you may decide to ignore his requests only to find him standing in a puddle.

The patient toddler learns to wait her turn. The patient eight-year-old can wait until Christmas morning to open presents. The patient teenager can wait until married to have sex. The patient parent can wait for the rebellious grown son to see the error of his ways and return to the values with which he was raised.

Sometimes we need to have patience when a desired result may not be achieved in the foreseeable future. Maybe the final outcome is delayed beyond a person's life-time. In 1945, Franklin Delano Roosevelt died less than a month before Germany surrendered in World War II. The possibility of his death did not alter his resolve in dealing with the conflict around the world. In ancient times, it took 115 years to build the Parthenon, a temple on the Acropolis in Athens (I think it's safe to say that its architect did not see his work completed). The patient person lives in the moment and can enjoy simple pleasures. He is in control, inclined to act his best regardless of the circumstances.

"The lab results won't be available until Monday." "We're home free if there is no reoccurrence in the next five years." "He is still missing." The patient person can hear any of these statements and remain in control. They realize that not being patient does little good and can make a dreadful situation worse. Patience allows them to make good decisions and be a source of strength and consolation to others.

Patriotism

Expressing love for your country,
honoring its values,
and being willing to serve it

Viewing your country as an
extension of your family

SEEDS TO PLANT: Be able to sing every word of the Star Spangled Banner.

WEEDS TO PULL: Don't walk, talk, eat, or move when you hear the
National Anthem.

FAMILY RULE: Respect family, community, and country.

W e mutually pledge to each other our lives, our fortunes and our sacred honor" is the last line of the Declaration of Independence. This notion seems almost incomprehensible more than two centuries later, and that's a crying shame.

Patriotism became uncool during the civil unrest of the 1960s and the Vietnam era. But public emotions change. The Desert Storm conflict in 1991 and even the recent release of the movie *Saving Private Ryan* resulted in a resurgence of patriotic emotions—though not to the level of what our founding fathers thought appropriate. Some people believe that flag waving, unabashed exuberance for our country in some ways clouds over the nation's past and current failings. But patriotism is not directed at our shortcomings. Its purpose is to honor the principles and spirit on which America was built. Patriotism allows us to focus on what as a nation and as individuals we can be. During the great World Wars, neighborhoods in large cities were clearly defined ethnic hubs—many nationalities, different languages. When the wars came, we were all Americans and what we had or hoped to have was in great peril. Our parents and grandparents responded and saved the world. They didn't lose sight of the fact that if you strive to make your country the best it can be, you will at the same time work to embody all it stands for.

Patriotism begins with loyalty in our homes and extends to our communities, our states, and finally to our country. And our patriotism extends beyond our borders. We avoid nationalism by respecting the rights of other countries. By acknowledging the noble intentions of other nations, we share the riches of America's sacred ideals.

We make much better decisions for the future when we know and honor our past. We have to study the sacrifices made by the Americans who have come before us, the issues they wrestled with. It's easy to become cynical when we see the grave injustices around us, but we have to show reverence for our national symbols. People who place their hands over their hearts during the Pledge of Allegiance and remove their hats when they hear the Star Spangled Banner will probably show respect to their spouses, their neighbors, and strangers walking down the street. They will vote, they won't litter, and they will volunteer for civic causes. These may be modest efforts, but they are still a tribute to our founding fathers and what they left us.

Peacefulness

Maintaining an amiable and calm demeanor that reflects a deep sense of well-being

SEEDS TO PLANT: Pick your battles.

WEEDS TO PULL: No temper tantrums.

FAMILY RULE: Express yourself calmly and gently.

P eacefulness is an inward quality that is reflected outwardly for all the world to see. It comes more easily to some people who are blessed with a temperament that craves harmony. If we are striving to have peacefulness in our lives, then we need to work on serenity and justice. Serenity results in inner peace and justice results in peaceful interpersonal relationships. A speaker at the United Nations once said, "If you want peace, work for justice."

My son Sam is by nature my most peaceful, composed child. He avoids arguments, is the first to look for peaceful situations, and cares deeply how other people feel. No, he is not for sale because when you're a mother of five, a child like him is a godsend. His temperament needs a little reinforcement of fortitude, so I am glad, but surprised, to see him occasionally be stubborn enough to dig in his heels. I resist the urge to take advantage of his agreeable nature, even though it makes my life easier. I don't want him to feel that he cannot assert himself. Being peaceful does not mean being passive, as Gandhi, the nonviolent leader in India, taught us.

In trying to be an agent of peace, some people develop the idea that the peace of the world somehow depends on them, and this can make them apprehensive. This anxiety erodes their peace of soul and can result in a variety of ailments. Sooner or later, an unexpected upheaval can take place within them that undoes the whole atmosphere of peacefulness.

A strong sense of justice is the foundation of virtuous peacefulness. We all have to be willing to take a stand, in a climate of rational discussion and compromise, for our own sake and for the sake of others. It can require having the self-control and self-assurance to yield control to others on negotiable, flexible issues.

Many times at home, I lose my temper because I want my family to know how strongly I feel about something. I want them to know how upset I am. This tends to become a habit because it gets results and I know my family will tolerate it. Still, it deteriorates the household atmosphere and is poor role-modeling. I've found the secret to avoid this. We all manage to control ourselves in public. If we can muster control publicly, we can do it privately. When there is a guest in my home, I show anger quietly and respectfully. If you imagine that the pastor or the school principal is in hearing distance, you're suddenly capable of great composure. Our families, more than anyone else, deserve this kind of peacefulness.

When Rebecca's children were very young and building toward a temper tantrum, she would make eye contact with them and say quietly, but firmly, "Use your words and use them nicely." When we use our words and use them nicely, peacefulness, tranquility reigns.

Perseverance

Keeping focused on and working toward
a worthwhile goal, even when doing so becomes
difficult, boring, or discouraging

SEEDS TO PLANT: Finish books, games, and projects.

WEEDS TO PULL: Don't lose sight of long-term commitments.

FAMILY RULE: Finish what you start.

Perseverance is a unique, all-purpose virtue. It is needed to get a job done well. It is needed to be faithful to commitments. It is needed to be steadfast in our beliefs. And it is needed to adhere to all other virtues. We especially need perseverance when we fail, or when a worthwhile objective hasn't yet been achieved. Perseverance in the laundry room allows you to change your clothes. Perseverance in the arena of high moral purpose allows you to change the world.

It's a good idea to practice perseverance in small matters just to develop the habit. After all, "the snail reached the ark by perseverance," as one wit observed. Finishing books, household projects, and even games can help us avoid being quitters. However, persevering for the sake of persevering can be foolhardy. The four cardinal virtues are very useful in discerning our objectives.

Consider, for example, a young mother who decides she wants to pursue a dream of running a marathon. A few weeks into her training, she realizes she is spending too much time and money. Her family seems to be suffering from her absence. She decides it isn't prudent or right to continue. Has she failed? No, she has made a noble decision. Pursuing a dream that is hurtful to the people around us is not virtuous. Winston Churchill agreed, telling us never, never to stop persevering, "except to convictions of honor and good sense."

Being faithful to our commitments to spouse and children requires long-term perseverance that can't be shelved because we have become distracted by a new goal. No greater good is served when we abandon our most basic obligations to pursue a morally neutral objective. When does the end justify the means in the application of perseverance?

A great symbol of perseverance for all the right reasons is found in the character of Atticus Finch in Harper Lee's novel *To Kill a Mockingbird*. If you haven't read the book or seen the movie in a while, consider doing it soon. The story is teeming with every kind of virtue. Atticus, you may recall, is a Depression era attorney in Maycomb, a small southern town. He decides to defend Tom Robinson, a black man who is wrongly accused of raping a poor white girl. He does this at great risk to himself and his children. He does this knowing, without a doubt, that he will lose the case and Tom Robinson will be found guilty. Still, he perseveres in his resolve to defend him—for the sake of Tom Robinson, for the sake of teaching his children, whom he loves, and for the townsfolk whom he believes to be misguided.

Tom Robinson is found guilty and shot when he panics and tries to escape. Many of the townsfolk revile Atticus for his effort. Eventually, his children are attacked. At the novel's conclusion, the reader doesn't think of Atticus as a failure. His children have learned to "walk around in someone else's skin" and his tireless perseverance to righteousness is illuminating and inspiring.

Piety

Being reverent and dutiful toward God, nature, your heritage, your parents, and others

SEEDS TO PLANT: Study your family history.

WEEDS TO PULL: Don't outlaw your in-laws.

FAMILY RULE: Remember where you came from.

Piety seems like a quaint little quality we might use to describe saints and other religious personalities. People sometimes think of it in a negative way, as a kind of religious showing off, but authentic piety is a virtue that calls for faithfulness in our relationship with others. Whether we recognize its value and impact or not, it has had an effect in our lives. Our respect for what has preceded us as related to our family or to history in general is apparent in how we live our lives. We cannot have a true appreciation of nature without it. It is an appreciation of greatness in ourselves and others.

Heritage is what we have inherited by birth, including our citizenship. Piety for our country comes to life in patriotism. We should value and celebrate our cultural or ethnic heritage in a personal way with our families and with others who share it with us. Piety is essentially a private virtue. While we should have respect for others and are entitled to the same from them for cultural and ethnic differences, we do not need anyone's acknowledgment to validate our identity. Piety itself makes this unnecessary.

Piety for nature is a human responsibility. We all have an obligation to not misuse or waste what we have in nature. If we aren't pious about nature, we really can't appreciate its splendor or our relationship to it. You don't have to be an environmental radical to be conscious of the natural order of this planet. Piety for earth is critical because it requires us to invest ourselves in nature for the sake of future generations.

Religious conviction can be our most profound source of piety. All religions that I know recognize free will. This alone is awe-inspiring. We need to learn about and understand our religious beliefs if we want to be truly pious, that is, to have a right relationship with the divinity.

If we are pious about our family, we will have a deep appreciation of our ancestors. To know our family history is to give us a great sense of identity. We should all spend time passing family lore on to our children. Doing so guarantees that our children will tell their children. To build up family piety requires us to maintain strong family ties. Parents should work hard to make sure their children appreciate both their paternal and maternal relatives, particularly grandparents and cousins. Sometimes, because of geography and even pettiness, either the paternal or maternal relatives are dominant in children's lives. This, in effect, cuts their birthright in half.

My parents would be the first to object if I showed up at their house on all the holidays because it would indicate that Bill's family was being neglected. Practically speaking, it can predispose a child to believe that when he or she gets married, they are supposed to choose a primary family. If the mother's side of the family is given preference, a son will likely believe that he is supposed to defer to his wife's family when he gets married.

Piety is not just reverence for what we have received from our ancestors. It also recognizes that we have an obligation to the people who will come after us. Consideration of what we leave to posterity reinforces our purposefulness in the present.

Politeness

Being gracious and civil so others feel comfortable and respected

SEEDS TO PLANT: Institute charm school.

WEEDS TO PULL: Ban coarse language.

FAMILY RULE: Mind your manners.

One of the things I miss most about the "olden days" is a gracious and civil manner. Even writing about this almost seems petty and condescending, but I can think of no other virtue that requires less effort and brings more immediate results.

Bad language is one of the most offensive things polluting our atmosphere for no better reason than so-called shock value. Ironically, it is so frequent that it is no longer shocking. I hear it on the street, in the grocery store, in movie-theater lines, and on the airwaves. Movies are among the worst offenders. Four-letter words that would have landed a twelve-year-old in detention are now being used routinely for a sitcom laugh or to sell wares on the radio.

Forgive me for nagging, but it seems to me when we lower the bar on language, all other simple rules of civility go out the window. Doors are not held open, gum is chomped in church, table manners are a fright, and little or no respect is granted to the elderly. Feminists are going to have a fit when I say this, but I blame women. When women start talking like sailors, the floodgates open to break all the simple rules of etiquette. I think they do this to be like the guys at the office or the plant. When men stop watching their language around women, it becomes such a habit that it doesn't occur to them to stifle it around children.

Like it or not, historically, women have always been the torchbearers of manners and politeness. Generally speaking, if we women decide to disregard common courtesy, you can bet many children are not being taught any sense of decorum. Are we all just too weary to make a fuss about what seems on the surface to be merely niceties? "Pick your battles" is a popular axiom for child rearing. I agree for the most part with regard to many aspects of relationships, but we have lost more than we realize when we capitulate all refinements of daily living.

Being polite and gracious toward everyone we encounter makes the world seem less harsh. Everyone from the cable guy to the fast-food cashier deserves to be treated with respect. Family members merit this consideration above all others. The world could use a refresher course in manners but the most we can hope to do is control the politeness barometer in our homes. We need to homeschool charm.

Prudence

Making decisions after gathering information
and considering consequences

Thinking things through before taking action

SEEDS TO PLANT: Hide a house key in your yard.

WEEDS TO PULL: Don't accept advertisements at face value.

FAMILY RULE: Look before you leap.

P rudence is sometimes called the master virtue because it is the only cardinal virtue that pertains strictly to the intellect. It's also called the "rudder" virtue because it "steers" all other virtues. It's a good thing that we have our children at home for 18 to 21 years because it takes a long time to fully develop prudence.

One of the first things we should know about prudence is that it is a reasoning process. Our society puts a huge emphasis on feelings. We use the word "feel" to describe our thoughts. "I feel Mr. Smith is a better candidate." Feelings can help us understand our thoughts, but we shouldn't base our decisions on them. They are too changeable and fickle for that! It isn't healthy to deny our feelings, but as I tell my kids, we are the bosses of our feelings.

When we base the decision-making process solely on feelings, we are in danger of making very rash decisions. "I quit my job because I don't feel the work is fulfilling." "I'm leaving my marriage because it's not making me happy." "I feel we are ready for sex." "I don't feel good about attending college in the fall." You get the picture.

Consider the prospect of marriage. My mother felt nervous about the way I approached relationships when I was in college. She thought I tended to romanticize things. She was right. I was always falling for the brooding Heathcliff types. She even wrote me saying, "You know, Daddy is no Lawrence Olivier, but I love him anyway." Her point was that I shouldn't judge the worthiness of a relationship only by how I felt. She taught me that we can have strong feelings for any number of people, and that we should judge with our heads as well as with our hearts.

After college, my roommates and I had fun with a point system for judging "worthy prospects." To gain WP status, the guys we dated had to maintain an eight or higher, on a scale from one to ten. Talk about objective! Drug use or prior marriages knocked any guy I dated out of WP status. A questionable work ethic or a dysfunctional family history was pause for serious consideration. The person I ended up marrying began as a nine (we both loved politics), dropped to a five (he tended to be a reluctant suitor), and rose to a ten (he is the most loyal human being I have ever known) by the time we married (five years after our first date).

I'm very serious about this. If you're not married, consider being as prudent as possible as you work your way to the altar. If you have children, teach them to be prudent in picking a spouse. Much unhappiness today is related to marriages that should have never taken place. Some of the worst social problems in this country are a result of these imprudent unions. Of course, you can't expect children to turn prudent at eighteen. Early on, a child should begin to use prudence in her decision-making process. What is my goal? How do I get there? Are there experts who can help me figure this out?

Prudence is looking before you leap. It's involves understanding and evaluating our actions and their consequences. As our thinking becomes more elaborate, it enables us to predict outcomes before having to suffer them. Prudence almost ensures making sound decisions. Prudence greatly increases the likelihood that our actions will serve a greater good.

Reflection

Deep consideration of your thoughts, words
and deeds, and how they relate to moral truth

SEEDS TO PLANT: Take a time-out.

WEEDS TO PULL: Don't ignore epiphanies.

FAMILY RULE: Sit and think.

Confucius, the ancient Chinese sage, said, "Look at this window: it is nothing but a hole in the wall, but because of it, the whole room is full of light." The process of reflection or contemplation can shed light on our perceptions, our reasoning, and our progress in virtue. Developing the habit of making time for reflection can shape our attitude, our world view. If we have a problem or concern, we should be determined to think it through, which will help us avoid fretting about it.

We don't have to sit on a rock yoga-style and hum to engage in reflection or contemplation. We don' have to be so disciplined that we set aside a special time and place to do it, though that would help. But we have to avoid distracting thoughts and focus on our concern fully. We use our memory to reflect on an event in our past, perhaps even a few hours earlier. We use our imagination to contemplate upcoming events. We use this time to remember important experiences we've had and contemplate how they will affect future experiences. Spending time in reflective prayer is an especially meaningful and fruitful way to worship God. Simply taking time to be thankful for blessings and the wonders of the world helps us to keep perspective.

Sometimes our anxious feelings will dissipate with proper perspective. We generally have to spend time thinking things through or doing an examination of conscience, on the front end to form a plan of action and on the back end to analyze how we could have done better. We can then determine what we will do differently in the future.

Epiphanies are illuminating moments when we are struck with insight or enlightenment. With the hectic lifestyles we live, it would be a shame to have an epiphany and not take the time to examine its meaning. We would miss an opportunity for life-altering realizations. We would miss panoramic views of our lives.

In his book *Living Simply in an Anxious World*, Robert J. Wicks writes, "How we perceive something is more relevant than what we perceive." If this is true, and I think it is, then we would be fools not to spend a fair amount of time in contemplation and reflection. Taking a few minutes a day for this is essential for clarity of purpose and peace of mind.

Repentance

Feeling regretful and seeking forgiveness
for a wrongdoing or mistake

Being willing to make amends

SEEDS TO PLANT: Take flowers to a friend you hurt.

WEEDS TO PULL: Don't resist consequences.

FAMILY RULE: Be willing to say "I'm sorry. How can I make amends?"

W hen children are very young, parents rarely feel angry with them, even for willful displays of temper. They get over this by the time they are four or so when real anger can flare up. As our children got older, Bill and I began our serious lectures about their misbehavior.

My oldest daughter would kind of swell up and act indignant when she was in trouble. She didn't seem contrite and this made us even angrier. When my oldest son got into trouble, he became an expert litigator, arguing our every point. Sometimes his ability to distract us with his legalism confused the issue. His "Perry Mason" approach made us even angrier. My second son tended to get a docile, almost vacant look on his face when he was in big trouble. We couldn't quite tell if we were reaching him and had to resist the urge to knock on his head and ask if anyone was home. His meek, compliant demeanor made us angrier. The youngest daughter would turn on the tears when she was in big trouble; she could flood the room with them. Her "water-works" approach made us angrier.

It occurred to me one day, before our fifth child was old enough to make us angry, that none of our children, to our displeasure, responded in an acceptable way. Were we picky because we were presented with four different styles, and none of them suited us? While discussing this, a light bulb went off and Bill realized that our children didn't know what they were supposed to do when they were in trouble. To our dismay, we realized we had never taught them how to respond appropriately. We had never thought about what we expected from them in this regard. We just wanted to feel as if we were reaching them and they were willing to repent.

"I'm sorry. What can I do to make amends?" became what we expected them to say. We accept their apologies, tell them how to make amends, and then hold them to it. With all their approaches they felt truly sorry, but it just didn't satisfy us or them, because being sorry is incomplete if you aren't willing to do something to make things right.

"I'm sorry. What can I do to make amends?" are powerful and disarming words. Think about the effect they could have on a teacher, an employer, an employee, a friend, parent, child, or spouse. To feel sorry, to express that sorrow, and to do whatever is necessary to right a wrong, is powerful contrition.

How do we make amends when there is nothing that we can do to alter a situation we are responsible for? My religion teaches me that nothing is unforgivable. If we do something really wrong or make a really stupid mistake, and there is no undoing it, what do we do? Our only alternative is to accept the consequences of our actions as willingly and gracefully as possible.

My husband and I will forgive our children anything, but we will do nothing to help them avoid the consequences. Our hope is that if they understand this while their mistakes are relatively inconsequential, they will be able to avoid having regrets of great consequence.

Resourcefulness

Being imaginative, creative, and inventive about finding solutions or coping with situations using every means available

SEEDS TO PLANT: Learn to brainstorm.

WEEDS TO PULL: Don't be easily discouraged.

FAMILY RULE: Be inventive in your thinking and doing.

1. clean shed
2. wash jugs
3. pick up labels
4. sort apples
5. ✓ supplies
6. repaint signs

In the novel *Gone with the Wind*, Scarlett O'Hara was resourceful. Unfortunately, for the people around her, she was not always virtuous. Resourcefulness in the hands of a right-minded person changes the world for the good. Resourcefulness in the hands of an unscrupulous person is cunningly self-serving. Directed to higher purposes, willfully determined people improve the world through discovery and inventiveness.

There seems to me to be a natural instinct in humans to be resourceful. Watch a two-year-old tenaciously try to get something he wants that he shouldn't have and you see willful determination. Notice a group of high-schoolers brainstorm how they might raise money to enter a band competition in a distant city. The Wright Brothers made the dream to fly a reality. Jonas Salk eradicated polio. Elisabeth Kubler-Ross advocated hospice care and helped bring dignity and comfort to our deathbeds. These people found answers because their resolve to conceive and implement change was not determined by the shortfalls of predecessors.

While resourcefulness requires us to think "outside the box"—being imaginative, creative, inventive—it does not mean that we reinvent the wheel when the wheel is

already there. We have to have the humility to learn, sometimes through brain-storming, that some resources are already available to us, and we shouldn't be too proud to use them or to build on them.

Resourcefulness is a wonderful quality to share with the world, but we also need to use it in our own family, in our own lives. When our personal world falls apart, when there is a family problem, we need to boost our resourcefulness—and teach our kids a lesson at the same time—in order to find what we need to survive. The willingness to do what you have to do is a quality of fortitude that is realistically applied through resourcefulness.

We should read up on the imaginative, creative, and inventive thinkers and doers of yesterday and today. We need to build on their resourcefulness and advance their brilliant innovations that can benefit humanity. No less important is the need to resourcefully draw on the means of our own inner strength, our virtues, imagination, and talents, to advance the righteous causes of our hearts and minds.

Respect

Being mindful that all people, including yourself,
are entitled to respect by reason of their humanity

Being a good steward of the
natural resources we all share

SEEDS TO PLANT: Appreciate and learn from senior citizens.

WEEDS TO PULL: Don't indulge in prejudicial thoughts or actions.

FAMILY RULE: Value life.

Recently, I was listening to a radio talk show that was debating the treatment of violent criminals by prison guards. Many people called in to say that criminals who had committed unspeakable crimes deserved anything they got from even sadistic guards. I don't consider myself soft on crime, but I couldn't disagree more.

Prisoners should have clean surroundings, nutritional food, hard work, and access to good books. Whether they are serving one year, life, or are on death row, they are entitled to humane treatment, to be looked upon with dignity, and to be treated courteously. Why? Every person possesses a fundamental dignity and deserves respect, not for what they did but for what they are. Second, I find it hard to believe that prison guards can spend the day cursing and bullying prisoners, turn it off, and go home and be loving to their families. Being hateful day in and day out sooner or later would coarsen, or brutalize, anyone.

As a virtue, respect does not depend on the quality or virtue of particular people: "This person is due fundamental respect as a human being; this person is not." It is a standard of behavior that is not dependent on anything but the fact that this person is a human being, whatever they may have done. When my children act disrespectfully toward classmates and try to justify it because of what the other kid did, I remind them that they are wrong for responding with disrespect for the person. It's awfully hard to cultivate respectful habits if we spend all our time judging who merits it and who does not.

Humility is the foundation of our respect for other people. It's why we must strive to eradicate racism and other prejudices in the world. How can we possibly have self-respect if we harbor bigotry? It impedes our capacity for love, which is the underlying principle of justice.

Respect must also be extended to our natural world, God's creation and our home. We don't have to be an environmental extremist, but we do have to be good caretakers of earth's resources for our own sake and for future generations. We should think of these resources not so much as inherited from our ancestors, but as borrowed from our descendants. Respect for life in general is what connects us with past and future generations, and dignifies the human experience.

Responsibility

Accepting the consequences of your actions whether the action was purposeful or accidental

Answering the call of duty

SEEDS TO PLANT: If it needs to be done, do it!

WEEDS TO PULL: No excuses!

FAMILY RULE: No complaining. No blaming. No whining.

D uc de Levis, a French soldier and writer, coined the phrase "noblesse oblige," which means "nobility has its obligations." If we hope to be noble, we must be responsible. In today's world, responsibility, being "answerable" or owning up to something, seems to be considered optional. Some high-profile professional athletes, who are perceived as role models because of their high visibility and physical abilities, resent being publicly criticized for their behavior, claiming that what they do off the playing field is their own business. A virtuous person steps forward and accepts responsibility, even if it is thrust upon him because of the position he holds. Not to do so is reprehensible.

"I didn't mean to" has been uttered on many occasions. The implication is that if some action has an unforeseen consequence, then he or she should not be held accountable. Not only are my children accountable for accidents, but I want them to get to the point where they avoid particular actions that lead to accidents in the first place. They are responsible for the lamp that was broken while they were playing catch with a baseball in the living room.

Certain professional sports people are by no means the only shirkers of responsibilities. It's fair to say that "baby boomers," generally speaking, are a whiny lot. Anything that interferes with their life plan is an assault on their "personal freedom." A major news magazine did a cover story on the so-called Mommy Track. The complaint was that after putting their lives on hold while raising children, women were then expected to look after aging parents. Here, in the dawn of the new millennium, government programs are being touted to offset the cost of caring for children and aging parents. One hundred years ago, people took care of the children they brought into the world and the parents who brought them into the world. It would have never occurred to our ancestors that the job belonged to someone else, least of all to the government. They didn't view life from the perspective of what they were entitled to or exempt from.

We could spend the rest of our lives citing reasons why we haven't done what we should. Reasons are of no value, nor are the excuses. Only infrequently may extenuating circumstances excuse us from our responsibilities, our obligations. I know I've used up my quota, as have my children.

Making peace with the fact that noblesse oblige is a reality that helps me do what I have to do. If I'm discouraged about the demands of my responsibilities, I remind myself that my responsibilities are a result of decisions I have made, of being blessed with a very full life. An empty life is not very demanding, but it isn't very rewarding, either.

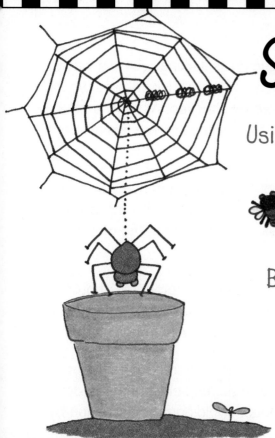

Self-Control

Using self-discipline to manage your thoughts, speech, temper, and actions

Being responsible and motivated

SEEDS TO PLANT: Do challenging tasks first.

WEEDS TO PULL: Do not give in to impulses.

FAMILY RULE: Act as you should, not as you feel.

I n the virtue-packed movie *Simon Birch*, Simon is talking with his buddy about something he wants to do and knows he shouldn't. His friend says, "If you feel like doing it, why don't you do it?" Simon seems shocked. As if it's a statement of personal policy he says, "What I feel like doing and what I do are two different things." What a novel idea!

Self-control is usually needed only after the application of prudence. You have already decided that you need to do something or refrain from doing it—that's when self-control comes into play. Now you need to muster the self-control, the discipline, to either do it or not do it.

Self-control also applies to our thoughts. We can't stop inappropriate thoughts from popping into our heads, but we shouldn't entertain harmful ideas or notions. Even if such thoughts were idle, wishful thinking, we would be wise to banish them.

With self-control, we can hold our tongue. Avoiding mean-spirited comments or forgoing the opportunity to spread a juicy bit of gossip requires self-control. So does swallowing our pride and apologizing for a hurtful deed. Avoiding procrastination by getting things done in a timely manner is a useful application of self-control, as is pushing ourselves away from the dinner table and not tossing that frivolous magazine into the grocery cart.

How many times a day do we rationalize our way out of some obligation because we just don't feel like following through? Self-control is essential if we want to be productive; it's critical if we are going to answer the call of duty.

This crucial virtue is easy to practice on a day-to-day basis. One good habit is to do challenging tasks first. Leaving undesirable tasks till last is risking never getting to them. Force yourself to do what you least like doing as soon as you can. Putting them off or avoiding them keeps us from getting more worthwhile things done or pursuing wholesome recreational activities. The guilt from not having done what we should hangs over us like a somber cloud.

Self-control is the incredible virtue that limits our behavior and bridles our passions. It helps us do what we should and resist what we shouldn't do. Self-control must be practiced daily in small ways so that it's "on call" when we're dealing with important issues. The disciplined family, the one with self-control, is much more likely to be a functional, loving family.

Sensitivity

Responding to the needs and feelings of others,
without being easily offended or overly impressionable

SEEDS TO PLANT: Be a good listener.

WEEDS TO PULL: Don't be thin-skinned.

FAMILY RULE: Understand how other people feel.

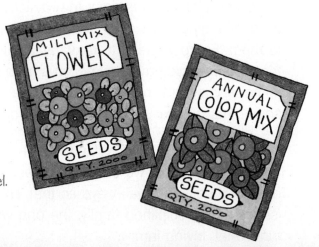

S ensitive people tend to be nurturing and loving, but this quality must be practiced with prudence, temperance, justice, and fortitude, or we risk becoming overly burdened and overly compliant.

Empathy is the ability to understand how other people feel and express this back to them. No other action is required when we empathize. Sometimes this is the most helpful thing we can do. Sensitive people need to resist the urge to fix everything for everyone; adults are grateful to know that we know how they feel. A child's self-confidence can be undermined when parents try to solve all their problems. Empathizing with them lets them know you know how they feel, but finding solutions is their job. If the problem is too big for them to solve, we should begin by suggesting alternatives. This will help them develop sound judgment. It's a huge relief, and realistic, to realize that we are not responsible for making everything right for our children all the time.

Sometimes very sensitive people overidentify with the people around them. We might even believe we have to embrace their point of view or take on their problems in order to prove our solidarity with them. This can make us ineffective and even indecisive. We just can't take on all the problems of the people around us. To believe we should is being presumptuous and overambitious.

Sensitive people also have to be wary about their feelings being hurt too easily. Being thin-skinned forces others to walk on eggshells when they are around them. If people's feelings are hurt too easily, and they show it, this will make others keep their distance, and their relationships will be superficial.

We need to be sensitive to strangers. This point was deeply appreciated when we were driving to the gravesite during the funeral for Bill's mother. We were touched by the cars that pulled over to the side of the road while our procession of cars passed. When we arrived at the cemetery, a crew of workers were making street repairs outside its entry. When our cars approached, they stopped their work, removed their hats, and were attentive until we were inside the gate. I wondered how many times that day they did that. I wondered how much longer it took them to get their work finished. And I still wonder if they know how moved we were by their sensitivity.

Sensitive people are a great source of comfort to those around them. They are tuned in to the needs and wants of others. They pick up signals of sadness or distress in another when other people may not. When sensitivity is tempered with prudence and justice, we can be helpful without hovering. Fortitude can keep us from being overly burdened and from carrying the weight of the world's problems on our shoulders.

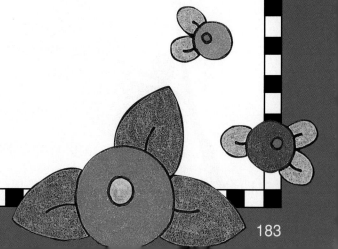

Serenity

Keeping a calm demeanor in
good times and bad

Facing hardships and bearing your
burdens with grace

SEEDS TO PLANT: Be a calm source of strength for others.

WEEDS TO PULL: Don't lose your balance.

FAMILY RULE: Believe that good will prevail.

Serenity helps us stay balanced, on an even keel, when things are going well or when they're going badly. This quality of being composed or tranquil keeps us from being giddy in good times and from being distraught or despairing in bad times. The deep-seated awareness that there will be good and bad times helps us maintain sound judgment and take the ups and downs of life in stride.

Why do we need serenity in good times? You've heard the stories of people who win the lottery and then their lives fall apart. When life seems perfect, we are likely to lose perspective and control of our priorities. With serenity, we can see the broad picture of life and stay focused on what is important. They say that when the going gets tough, the tough get going. The serene of spirit stay the course. Serenity allows them to remember where they are heading and keeps them from getting blown off course by difficulties and hardship.

What nonreligious people think of as a moral strength religious people believe is grace, a gift from God. In music, a grace note is not necessary to a melody but is added for embellishment. Without grace, life is plain and hard and without beauty. Serenity is beyond us in the absence of grace.

People gravitate to serene people, because they have a calming influence and inspire hope in difficult times. They appear to possess an aura of being in control. Owning and manifesting this quality will serve us and others well.

Simplicity

Presenting a true image of life by being genuine and honest

Keeping your behavior, motivations, and lifestyle uncomplicated

SEEDS TO PLANT: Make eye contact.

WEEDS TO PULL: Don't put on airs.

FAMILY RULE: Less is more.

Simplicity is a *Little House on the Prairie* state of mind. I always loved that show. Yes, I confess, I watched the TV show long before I read the books. To the best of my recollection, Laura Ingalls Wilder's classic stories were not required reading in the 1960s. They have been on my own children's required reading list, however, so I have since caught up with my children and read the stories with pleasure.

Any given episode—oops, I mean chapter—underscores this basic fact: Knowing who you are and what you stand for, working hard and making do with what you have, is what makes you a decent human being. Devotion to family, neighbor, church, and country is what we all should be about.

I'm not suggesting we turn the clock back to the nineteenth century. Having modern conveniences, miracle drugs, and going to the moon is not what keeps us from living the Little House life. Nor is it the availability of illegal drugs, sexually explicit and violent movies, MTV, or the Internet either. They just make it harder.

Do any of us think that penicillin and sexual promiscuity or indoor plumbing and credit card debt are packaged deals, essential elements of life? We can't turn off the

TV? We can't tell our children to stay home? And we can't tell the guy from First-whatever-bank that we can't afford and don't want any more credit?

We acquiesced, we submitted, and we capitulated to the turpitude of the twentieth century. We embraced both the wonders and the iniquities of society. But we can change all that right now. We can discern what will uncomplicate our lives and allow us to be simple in our outlook and way of life. Being simple-minded does not have to carry the negative meaning we give it. We can be simple-minded by having a few simple principles for living and not violating them for any reason. We can decide what we stand for, what we believe in, what we will teach our children, and what we will allow inside our homes. We can start right now. We don't have to form a committee, gather data, wait for laws to pass or courts to rule. We just do it. It is really that simple.

Sociability

Getting along with a variety of people in different settings, showing interest in their thoughts and feelings

Sharing your ideas in a modest way

Being attentive to the needs of others

SEEDS TO PLANT: Be a good listener.

WEEDS TO PULL: Avoid one-upmanship

FAMILY RULE: Give others the benefit of the doubt.

The ability to get along with others is essential in all walks of life. Strong social skills can make the difference between success and failure. The sociable person has the ability to connect with people in a very positive way. It's being willing, even eager, to make even chance or casual encounters as pleasant as possible. Long-term relationships spring from first encounters that have positive beginnings and are continued with a tone of basic congeniality.

If you are a sociable person, you are a comfortable person to be around because you are willing to share yourself with others. You have found the appropriate balance to do this without being intrusive or offensive. By doing so you risk rejection, but you know there is much to gain by connecting with others. Too many of us, for a variety of reasons, fail to make the effort.

Lest you think sociability is too self-serving to be a virtue, consider Iris, who has been a checkout clerk for at least the fifteen years I have been shopping at my neighborhood grocery store. I am among the customers who will stand in line a little longer at her register because I look forward to our little chats.

Iris knows my husband and all my children by name. She has soothed my colicky infants, distracted my whiny toddlers, and fussed over my insecure adolescents. Iris is a valued employee, but she doesn't get paid a commission on how many shoppers choose to check out at her register. It is just her habit to be sociable and agreeable. Because of this she has a positive impact on hundreds of people every week, which is a contribution to society worth noting. If you see the root-word similarity between "sociable" and "society," you also see why sociable people make for a pleasant society.

Teaching your child early in life to be sociable will help her maneuver more successfully through various childhood phases. Her peers will benefit from having a classmate who is mannerly, respectful, and congenial. Children well schooled in the virtue of sociability could certainly improve the emotional climate of middle schools across the nation.

Have you ever come across an adult whose good ideas and good intentions are discounted because he or she has obnoxious tendencies or poor inter-personal skills? Many times I've wanted to slip a copy of Dale Carnegie's classic book *How to Win Friends and Influence People* to someone who seems to be his own worst enemy. It should be required reading in every high school in America.

Sociability is having a genuine interest in other people and showing it by being civil and affable in their presence. Profound connections within our families, our neighborhoods, our nation, and around the world emanate from sociable relationships.

Temperance

Practicing restraint in your thoughts, words, and deeds so that you are a well-rounded person

SEEDS TO PLANT: Resolve to walk thirty minutes a day.

WEEDS TO PULL: Don't have second helpings.

FAMILY RULE: Know when to say when.

C arrie Nation became famous during the temperance movement, the purpose of which was to get people to abstain from drinking alcoholic beverages. She was arrested thirty times for using a hatchet to destroy bars and other places where drinks were served. One could say that Carrie Nation was intemperately temperate.

Temperance, a cardinal virtue, is moderation in everything so that we are rational and self-possessed individuals. It assists us in our passions. While it is often associated with our base appetites, temperance really enables us to be stable and effective in our pursuits. "Selfless self-preservation," Joseph Pieper said of temperance. And before him, philosophers over the centuries have urged us to moderate our appetites.

Before and after Carrie Nation, human beings have wanted what they want. It may seem worse now, but it has always been a struggle for human nature to resist the belief that if some is good, then more is better. We've always had trouble buying into the idea that less is more. In the last half of this century, we have been able to have more of everything if we wanted it. The current rate of consumer debt suggests that, generally speaking, we feel entitled to what we desire. It is our responsibility to resist greed and impulsive consumption and acquisition, even when the advertising industry does everything it can to encourage us to buy, buy, buy and pushes the desires of our heart toward flagrant consumerism.

Temperance is about having a balanced view of life. It sets us apart from the animal kingdom where physical urges and appetites are instinctual. (How interesting that animals do not overeat or overdrink, and copulate only for the sake of offspring!) Sadly, our inability to be temperate reduces our ability to enjoy many of life's pleasantries.

Temperance is highly susceptible to habit. We can be less indulgent with eating, drinking, and pleasure seeking, moderate our moods, and avoid discontent with applied temperance. Virtually all of our dispositions can be properly regulated with the practice of it. Twenty-one days to a better me just by using temperance to readjust my natural inclinations—what a deal! And in the process, by my example, demonstrate to my children that moderation should be their lifelong companion. I should start today.

Tolerance

Enduring the trials and tribulations of daily living

Respecting the rights of others

SEEDS TO PLANT: Try to be understanding.

WEEDS TO PULL: Don't put down others.

FAMILY RULE: Agree to disagree on some issues.

The very best training for respecting the rights of other people takes place at home where family members learn to work together, in spite of differences, to accomplish a wide variety of individual and collective objectives. A tolerant atmosphere in our homes means we avoid criticism, put up with inconvenience, and don't make a point of always making a point. We don't have to make an issue of every little thing.

Sometimes when I get annoyed by a minor skirmish, one of my kids will remind me that arguments are just a part of life. My overreaction to quarrels and disagreements between kids disturbs the atmosphere of our home more than a small dispute over whose turn it is to clean out the dishwasher.

Getting along with others depends on being able to agree to disagree. Helping children learn to see each other's point of view fosters understanding. It doesn't mean giving in or losing the battle. But understanding one another does make it easier to declare a truce or to find a position of compromise.

We live in a country of countless ideologies, opinions, and beliefs. The law of the land requires me to tolerate the rights of other people who oppose everything I stand for. I have the right, though, and in some cases the moral obligation to express my views, try to change people's minds, or work within the legal system to change the laws of the land. Being intolerant doesn't help my cause and can serve to further alienate people from my position on an issue. I need to be able to rationally present my case, if I want people to understand my thinking and consider the merits of where I stand. Tolerant people are much more persuasive than intolerant people.

Family life is the ideal place in which to hone these skills. There are certainly enough opportunities to school ourselves in toleration.

Trustworthiness

Being honest and reliable with family, friends, institutions, and yourself

Being dependable and ready to respond to the needs of others

SEEDS TO PLANT: Follow through on commitments.

WEEDS TO PULL: No lying.

FAMILY RULE: Say what you mean, and mean what you say.

Trustworthiness is a big virtue, encompassing honesty, dependability, and truthfulness. Our words and actions should be consistent with our thoughts and intentions. I know as well as anyone how easy it is to fall into the habit of telling little white lies from time to time. Such fibs make our life easier and, before you know it, "from time to time" can become almost any time. Children tell lies to avoid punishment; adults tend to tell them to avoid confrontation, uncomfortable situations, and inconvenience. Sometimes we lie without speaking. If we are trying to give someone a false impression, to mislead the person by our demeanor or gestures, it's a lie all the same.

Is there ever justification for a lie? Sometimes prudence dictates that some things are better left unsaid. We are not obligated to share our every thought, but we do need to be kind. If a person is bold enough to ask us about a private matter, assuming we are not on a witness stand, it's reasonable to be evasive.

Reliability, the quality that tells people they can count on you, is a part of trust-worthiness. You must do what you say you are going to do. Once you have a reputation for not following through, for not keeping your word, it is very hard to undo the impression you've made, your reputation for being unreliable. I'm blessed with many friends

I can rely on. Not only do they always do what they say they are going to do, but they are available anytime I need something. Sometimes they pop up to do for me what I never would have asked them to do. Reliability like that deepens friendships.

When Rebecca and I hardly knew each other and I was expecting my fourth baby, she heard from Abby, my oldest daughter, that I was under the weather. One day, instead of just dropping Abby off at my door, she swooped up my two preschoolers and, hours later, returned the kids, fed, bathed, and ready for bed. That was the beginning of a wonderful friendship that extended to a business partnership nine years later. Our relationship is built on trust. How meaningful can a relationship be without trust?

We must also be able to trust ourselves, our intuitions and instincts. We can't reason prudently if we deceive ourselves, aren't honest with ourselves. None of the cardinal virtues are useful if they aren't based on truth. When we look around and see dishonest, unreliable, and generally untrustworthy people getting ahead, or at least going unpunished, it can be discouraging. We should guard our hearts against discouragement and cynicism. Instead, we can feel sympathy for those who build their lives on falsehood and celebrate the authentic trustworthiness of our own lives.

Wisdom

Knowledge of life gained from study, experience, and moral authority

SEEDS TO PLANT: Apply truth as you know it.

WEEDS TO PULL: Never forsake righteousness.

FAMILY RULE: Seek wisdom and love.

We are all philosophers from the moment we begin to think. Our philosophical first steps are apparent when we begin to ask questions about the things we see: What is it? What makes it what it is? How does it work? Why is it the way it is? Where did it come from? What if. . . ? The word "philosophy" means love of wisdom. Wisdom comes to us very slowly over the years through reflection on our experiences, our reading, our conversations; through adversity and moments of heightened awareness. We have to pursue it deliberately over the course of a lifetime, and we can never stop trying to acquire it. Like humility, once we think we have it we have lost it.

We must never stop learning. Reading good books and soaking up information and ideas that we don't even know we need has to be a never-ending process. Even with an I.Q. of a gazillion, you always need more information and more reflection to satisfy your desire to understand new ideas—if you want to grow in wisdom.

Life's lessons come from life's experiences, either our own or other people's, and reflecting on them deepens our insights into human nature, into the reasons for why things are the way they are. It is folly not to observe and learn from the mistakes and triumphs we experience day in and day out.

If we want to grow in wisdom, we have to have a moral authority or moral code outside ourselves to live by. To travel the long road toward wisdom without it is a form of egotism that will have us traveling in a circle, never arriving at authentic wisdom. If we want to grow in wisdom, we must realize that our most basic desires, the desires of our heart, must be truth, righteousness, and love. These three elements belong to wisdom, and there is no true wisdom without them.

About the Authors

Christina Keffler (right) and **Rebecca Donnelli** (left) and illustrator **Suzanne Etman** (middle) are a trio of moms who live in the Dallas area and speak frequently to large and small groups about teaching virtues to children. They are the creators of a calendar by the same name. They have been featured in a variety of print media stories, notices, and reviews both locally and statewide.

The Garden of Virtues book and calendar have been recommended by the following highly-regarded individuals:

"Proper values are the key to successful living. They are the most valuable legacy we can leave our children. The Garden of Virtues is a useful aid in passing life's hard-learned lessons on to the next generation."—**General Colin L. Powell**, USA (Ret.)

"In an era of moral confusion, the Garden of Virtues helps families plant the values necessary to cultivate the next generation of positive and productive young people."—**Senator Bob Dole**

"The Garden of Virtues calendar is a much needed, easy-to-use method of teaching virtue. These are indispensable qualities for the successful rearing of a child. [The calendar is] a good idea whose time has come."—**Zig Ziglar**, Author and Motivational Speaker

"A wonderful way to help children and families grow ethically as caring and committed persons." —**Rabbi Sheldon Zimmerman**, President, Hebrew Union College, Jewish Institute of Religion

"The best family calendar ever!"—**Ann Applegarth**, Catholic Parent Magazine

"I give the parents in my classes a Garden of Virtues calendar. It is a great resource for them. The activities are fun, easy to do, and teach important lessons."—**Joan Roberts**, Parenting Co-chair, Family Outreach

"The Garden of Virtues provides parents and teachers with an easy-to-use tool to teach some of the most essential elements. It is a unique and effective way to implement activities at home and across the curriculum at school . . . reinforcing the language and behaviors we all strive to teach." —**Helen Allison**, M.Ed.

"Garden of Virtues is bright and charming for home use. . . at a time when we lament the loss of a sense of virtue in our society. Garden of Virtues is a refreshing return to fostering basic principles." —**Msgr. John Bell**, Chaplain, University of Dallas

Plant Seeds of Goodness Every Day by ordering the
Garden of Virtues Wall Calendar

Features:

- Simple Definitions

- 4-7 Specific Habits

- Family Rule

Plus over **200** hands-on activities ideal for families and classrooms.

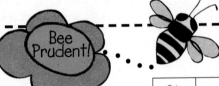

Bee Prudent!

To order: Send Check or Money Order to

Homegrown, Inc.
2305 Springwood Lane
Richardson, Texas
75082

(972) 907-2442

Qty.	Item	Cost	Total
	Calendar	$11.95	
	Shipping & Handling		$3.75
	Subtotal		
8.25% sales tax (TX residents only)			
	Total amount enclosed		

Visit our web site WWW.virtuescalendar.com and charge it!

Name_____

Address_____

City_____ State_____ Zip_____

☐ Please add my name to your mailing list!   ☐ Please send fund-raising information.

✂